it hurts you inside

children talking about smacking

Carolyne Willow and Tina Hyder

Save the Children

The National Children's Bureau (NCB) works to identify and promote the well-being and interests of all children and young people across every aspect of their lives.

NCB is a registered charity which encourages professionals and policy makers to see the needs of the whole child and emphasises the importance of multidisciplinary, cross-agency partnerships. It has adopted and works within the UN Convention on the Rights of the Child and according to NCB stated values and principles.

It collects and disseminates information about children and promotes good practice in children's services through research, policy and practice development, membership, publications, conferences, training and an extensive library and information service.

Several Councils and Fora are based at NCB and contribute significantly to the breadth of its influence. It also works in partnership with Children in Scotland and Children in Wales and other voluntary organisations concerned for children and their families.

Save the Children is the UK's leading international children's charity, working to create a better future for children.

In a world where children are denied basic human rights, we champion the right of all children to a happy, healthy and secure childhood. We are particularly committed to listening to, and learning from, children and speaking out about the problems they face.

We use our global project work and research to lobby for changes that will benefit all children, including future generations.

We oppose violence of any sort against children – whether physical or mental – and campaign to end all violence to children. In our projects worldwide, we work on initiatives to prevent violence. We also support children to recover from violence.

We believe that children have the same right to protection from violence as adults. We are lobbying for the UK law to be changed to outlaw physical punishment of children.

© Splodge illustrations by D A Orli, Nottingham.
Published by National Children's Bureau Enterprises, the trading company for the National Children's Bureau, 8 Wakley Street, London EC1V 7QE. Registered Charity Number 258825.
Published in association with Save the Children.
ISBN 1 900990 44X
© National Children's Bureau/Save the Children, 1998.
Printed by Billingham Press Limited.

Contents

Acknowledgements

Many people helped us carry out this project. Our biggest thanks goes to the 76 children who generously shared their ideas, experiences and views with us. Thanks also to the Joseph Rowntree Charitable Trust and Save the Children who supported us financially. We are grateful to all those who meticulously commented on previous drafts of this report, especially to Priscilla Alderson, Sophie Laws and Marjorie Smith. Finally our special thanks to the painstaking work of Sabina Collier, Denise Hollingberry and Anita Udoh, who typed the transcripts, and to David Orli for creating Splodge.

About the authors

Carolyne Willow ran the Children's Participation Programme at the National Children's Bureau until September 1998. Her previous publications include *Children's Rights and Participation in Residential Care* (National Children's Bureau Enterprises); *Hear! Hear! Children and Young People's Democratic Participation in Local Government* (Local Government Information Unit); and *On the Rights Track: Guidance for local authorities on establishing children's rights and advocacy services* (CROA and Local Government Association).

Tina Hyder is a development worker in the London Younger Children's Team at Save the Children Fund. She is co-author of *On Equal Terms: Involving parents in early years settings* (Save the Children Fund and National Early Years Network); *An Equal Future: Anti-sexist strategies in the early years* (Save the Children Fund and National Early Years Network); and *Refugee Children in the Early Years* (Refugee Council and Save the Children).

1. Foreword

I am delighted to introduce this unique report into young children's views and experiences of smacking. It is essential that young children are heard by adults, and this report powerfully shows the strength of feeling among children.

This report confirms my personal view as a parent that smacking children is wrong. One of the main reasons I am against smacking is that it sends a very early message that our society approves of violence. I am also totally unconvinced of its effectiveness as a deterrent or corrective for bad behaviour. In my experience children are often repeatedly smacked for doing the same thing. Certainly when I was at school, the same children would be smacked or caned over and over again.

I also believe smacking is symptomatic of a lack of respect for children's rights. Indeed, in my view, it is bullying of the worst kind – a large powerful adult hitting a small defenceless child who could not inflict the same amount of pain on his or her assailant. We know now of the prevalence of child abuse. I believe that as a society, our acceptance of smacking may at best lead us to overlook or not report physical abuse and that at worst it sends a sign that we condone such abuse. A clear and legal statement that *no* kind of smacking is acceptable, would I believe, send a powerful message to the contrary.

I think this needs to go hand in hand with an educational programme for parents and parents to be. As I discovered, parenting is a complex and challenging process but there are other ways to discipline a child – as the children in this report clearly testify.

If we are serious about reducing the levels of violence in our society, we must prepare children with the attitudes and skills to tackle problems, difficulties and frustrations in a non-violent way. Young children learn about relationships from the people they live with, and parents are the most significant people in most of their lives. We cannot begin to tackle violence in our society until we seriously address violence against children in the home.

I urge adults everywhere to carefully read this report and digest what children are telling us. The 76 children who took part in this consultation project were optimistic that smacking children can be stopped. I hope we can share their optimism and take all steps possible to ensure they no longer have to endure levels of violence which – if directed at adults – would provoke a public outcry.

Lorraine Heggessey

Lorraine Heggessey, Parent and Head of BBC Children's Programmes
Lorraine Heggessey is writing in a personal capacity.

2. Introduction

For too long one voice has been missing in the debate about children and physical punishment – the voice of children themselves, and particularly younger children.

This report is especially welcome in that it provides young children – five, six and seven-year-olds – with the opportunity to express their feelings about being smacked, share their views about smacking, and present their ideas about preventing smacking. It makes poignant reading. Its purpose is not to shock, but to encourage action to reduce violence in our communities, starting in the home. It is not an attack on parents. Parenting is a difficult job, not helped by the lack of clarity on what is or is not acceptable or harmful to children.

This consultation project was a unique exercise in listening to young children talking about a subject most adults find difficult. We rarely – if ever – hear from young children on issues like this. Yet who could have a more important contribution to make?

For the National Children's Bureau and Save the Children this report is an important affirmation of Article 12 of the United Nations Convention on the Rights of the Child, to which the UK has been a signatory since 1991: a child capable of forming his or her own views has *'the right to express those views freely in all matters affecting the child, the views of the child being given due weight in accordance with the age and maturity of the child'*.

As well as the challenge of listening to young children and taking their views into account, this report presents a further challenge: how can we respond to what children are saying, and ensure that our youngest citizens have the same rights to protection as everyone else?

It is important to remind ourselves that children are the only group of citizens in the UK who can legally be hit. Current laws in the UK are founded on a concept of 'reasonable chastisement' from the 19th century. Children were then seen as possessions of parents rather than as individual people in their own right. The modernisation of the law in this area is necessary.

The extent of physical punishment of children is more widespread than many people think. Recent research commissioned by the Department of Health (Smith, 1995) found that two thirds of babies were hit in their first year of life; up to a third of young children under seven were hit by their parents more than once a week; more than a third of children experienced severe punishment at the hands of their parents at some time, and a fifth had been hit with an implement. This level of violence would undoubtedly be illegal if directed at adults so why not for children? Such violent acts also signify the beginning of a cycle of behaviour which legitimises violence as an acceptable response to human conflict and frustration.

It is not easy to distinguish between beating on the one hand and smacking on the other. Smacking *can* lead to and legitimise serious physical abuse. Many perpetrators of violence against children openly declare that they had the right to do what they did, or say they merely *went a bit too far*. The law currently encourages a dangerous confusion.

Eight other European countries have already taken the step of outlawing corporal punishment of children in all circumstances – the result has not been a surge of prosecutions or intervention in families but a shift in attitudes and behaviour, backed up by positive family support and education.

In the UK we now have the opportunity to take a similar step. The Government is committed to consult on reform of the law on parental discipline, and in 1999 will be reporting on its progress towards implementation of the United Nations Convention on the Rights of the Child. Crucially the Government will be expected to report on the steps it has taken to implement Article 19 of the Convention, which states that children should be protected from *'all forms of physical or mental violence'*.

It is possible for Britain to comply with the Convention and outlaw smacking, as indeed it proved possible to outlaw violence against women within marriage, physical punishment of servants, and, most recently, corporal punishment of children in schools.

Children have waited at the back of the queue long enough. They are our smallest and most vulnerable citizens yet they are the only people who the law sanctions being hit. This report powerfully shows that young children have important views and feelings on the subject. The time has come to listen to what children are telling us, and act to give them the same legal protection as adults.

Barbara Hearn
Practice Development Director
National Children's Bureau

John Errington
Programmes Director – England
Save the Children Fund

3. Executive summary

Why consult children about smacking?

When the Government announced that it intended to consult the public on reforming the law on physical punishment at the end of 1997, this presented a challenge to our two organisations: how could we ensure young children contributed to the debate?

The National Children's Bureau and Save the Children have been working with and on behalf of young children for many decades, and we are both fully committed to ensuring that children can express their views in all matters which affect them. Given that most physical punishment is directed at young children – including babies and toddlers – (Newson and Newson, 1989; Smith, 1995), we believe it is essential that young children contribute to public debates on this issue. We decided to focus our discussions with children on smacking as this particular aspect of physical punishment is so commonly and forcefully defended.

Young children's views are seldom sought on matters which affect them as a group. One of the primary reasons appears to be the perceived difficulty in finding out what children think. Underlying this is the sense that children are not competent; that their views, thoughts, wishes and feelings do not have as much weight as those of adults. Berry Mayall (1994) in Morrow (1996) outlines some of the perceived problems of carrying out research with or consulting young children:

> '[It is assumed that] ...*children can't tell truth from fiction; children make things up to please the interviewer; children do not have enough experience or knowledge to comment on their experience, or indeed to report it usefully; children's accounts are themselves socially constructed, and that what they say in conversation or tell you if you ask them is what they have been told by adults.*'

She continues to explain that all these points can equally apply to adults.

The challenge is to understand and prepare for the difficulties inherent in carrying out consultations with young children rather than simply cut them out of these processes altogether.

Proceeding with caution

Before embarking on this consultation project we knew just how sensitive and provocative the subject of smacking is for adults. We were unsure how young children would view the subject and so approached it with the same level of caution and sensitivity required by adults. We wanted to ensure that the particular needs of young children were addressed. From previous experience, we knew the questions and process had to be *just right* if we were to successfully engage the interest and attention of children. Appropriate methods to elicit and record young children's views were considered carefully: we wanted to be sure that children could talk freely and openly about smacking, and that they would not be influenced by adult views on the subject. That is why the two project workers who carried out this work – both experienced in consulting children – decided from the outset that children would not be informed about our organisations' considered view that smacking is wrong. Children were told *they* were the experts on smacking, and that our organisations were seeking their views alone. The project workers also stressed the importance of children giving their own individual thoughts and responses rather than copying their friend's answers.

What we did

During July and August 1998 we carried out 16 small group discussions with 76 five to seven-year-olds (there was one four-year-old) in six schools and two summer play schemes. One school was an independent fee-paying school, another was a Church of England school, and the rest had diverse catchment areas. In 14 of the 16 discussions a teacher or other school/play scheme representative was present throughout. Parents were fully briefed in advance and gave written permission for children to take part (see Appendix A). Children's consent was obtained at the beginning of the discussions, when they were advised that they could opt out at any stage of the proceedings (either by leaving the room or not answering particular questions). Only four children – all five-year-olds – decided not to complete the group discussion.

Each of the school groups were divided according to age so that five, six and seven-year-olds were questioned separately. The two groups from the summer playschemes were mixed.

Who we listened to

We listened to slightly more girls (57%) than boys (43%); 32% were five-years-old, 32% six years and 36% were aged seven. One child was four-years-old.

Twenty per cent of the children were from black and minority ethnic communities while 18% of the children said they needed special help in school.

Fifty per cent of those who took part live in the South of England while 26% live in the Midlands and 24% in the North of England. The majority (51%) of the children were living with both birth parents and siblings.

What we asked

To assist our discussions with children we commissioned a community artist to produce a story book (see Appendix B) with the central character (later to become *Splodge*) to whom children could relate. Splodge was introduced to children as not knowing much about our world. To help Splodge understand smacking, a series of questions were put to groups of children, who answered questions in turn.

Splodge's questions:

- **Who knows what a smack is?**
- **Why do you think children get smacked?**
- **Who usually smacks children?**
- **Where do children usually get smacked?**
- **What does it feel like to be smacked?**
- **How do children act after being smacked? How do adults act after they have given a smack?**
- **Adults smack children but why don't children smack adults? Children smack each other but why don't adults smack each other?**
- **When you are big do you think you will smack children?**
- **Do you know anybody who doesn't like smacking? Who thinks it is wrong to smack?**
- **How can we stop children being smacked?**

The initial story book was piloted among under eight-year-olds and some amendments made to both the illustrations and the text. Although we describe our interaction with children as 'discussions' in reality they were more like question and answer sessions. Children did discuss questions among themselves but our role was restricted to questioning and clarifying points where there was possible ambiguity.

What we heard

This consultation exercise has nine major messages:

Children talking about smacking – the main messages
- Children defined smacking as hitting; most of them described a smack as a hard or very hard hit.
- Children said smacking hurts.
- The children said children are the main people who dislike smacking followed by parents, friends and grandparents; the vast majority of the children who took part thought smacking was wrong.
- The children said children respond negatively to being smacked, and adults regret smacking.
- The children said parents and other grown ups are the people who mostly smack children.
- The children said they usually get smacked indoors and on the bottom, arm or head.
- The children said the main reasons children are smacked include: they have been violent themselves; they have been naughty or mischievous; they have broken or spoiled things; or because they have disobeyed or failed to listen to their parents.
- The children said children do not smack adults because they are scared they will be hit again; adults do not smack each other because they are big and know better, and because they love and care about each other.
- Half the children involved in this consultation exercise said they will not smack children when they are adults; five-year-olds most often said they will not smack children when they are big.

The National Children's Bureau and Save the Children believe these compelling messages will have greatest impact on three groups of people: parents; children's organisations and professionals working with children; and the Government. To parents the message from this report is clear – smacking hurts, and smacking harms relationships between parents and children.

The children we listened to suggested many activities which adults could pursue to stop or reduce smacking. A five-year-old girl proposed that adult relatives could physically stand in the way of a parent who is attempting to hit a child. Many children described educational initiatives – in their own words these included putting up posters, sending parents letters or making a news broadcast to tell parents that smacking is wrong. Clearly there is a role here for children's organisations; this report certainly adds to our organisations' determination in advocating the right of children to full legal protection from assault.

Finally, we expect this report to have impact at Government level. At the very least we expect the Government to increase its general efforts to ensure young children are involved in a meaningful way in other areas of policy development.

This report offers adults and the Government a window through which they can clearly see the distress, pain and hurt caused to children by the continued social and legal acceptance of smacking. The National Children's Bureau and Save the Children would like to see steps taken to ensure that our youngest citizens have the same legal rights to protection from any form of assault as older people. This will not only – over time – greatly reduce children's suffering, it will also substantially improve relationships between parents and children.

4. Setting the context

Several factors precipitated this consultation exercise.

The Government's consultation on law reform

In November 1997 the Government announced its plan to review the law which allows 'reasonable chastisement' of children, and said it would consult on how to change the law. The Government was responding to a Report of the European Commission of Human Rights on a case involving the repeated caning of a young English boy by his stepfather. The Commission found unanimously that the beating breached Article 3 of the European Convention on Human Rights ('no one shall be subjected to inhuman or degrading treatment or punishment'), and that domestic law, for which the Government was responsible, did not prevent such breaches. The stepfather, who did not deny the beatings, was acquitted by a British jury in 1994 who accepted the defence of 'reasonable chastisement'.

The Government condemned the treatment of the boy as 'cruel, inexcusable and having no place in a civilised society', accepted that the law relating to parental discipline must be reviewed; and publicised its plans to issue a consultation paper on law reform 'to reach a wide consensus on the best way forward'. It stated: *'Degrading and harmful punishment inflicted on children can never be justified. It is right that the common law defence of 'lawful correction' or 'reasonable chastisement' should not be used to excuse it'*. But its immediate response also said that this particular case had *'... nothing to do with parents who exert discipline by smacking their children when they misbehave. We respect that right. The overwhelming majority of parents know the difference between smacking and beating'*.

The European Court on Human Rights delivered its unanimous judgement, at Strasbourg on 23 September 1998, that Article 3 of the European Convention on Human Rights had been violated in the above case. Once again the Government condemned the actions of the stepfather but persisted in stating that the case had nothing to do with smacking. Paul Boateng, junior health minister at the time, noted that, *'this Government believes in parental discipline. Smacking has a place within that, and our law will not change in order to outlaw [it]'*.

As the children who took part in this consultation exercise make clear, it is difficult to make straightforward distinctions between 'smacking', 'slapping', 'beating' or 'whacking'. What they have in common is that all, if directed at an adult, or even threatened, potentially constitute a criminal assault.

Adults frequently underestimate the force and impact of smacking. From a grown adult's point of view, a smack may appear to involve minimal force; from a small child's perspective smacking can be a forceful blow inflicting severe pain. It is hard for adults to imagine being hit by someone twice our size but that is exactly what happens when adults smack children. We know that parents can cause as much damage to a young child with the open hand as with some implements: picture a toddler being slapped by a parent wearing a ring, or a hit on a child's head which makes her lose her balance and fall onto a hard surface. A leaflet, jointly commissioned by the Department of Health and the NSPCC, advises parents: 'Remember – it's NEVER OK to shake or smack a baby'. The Health Education Authority advises against smacking in its pamphlet sent to all pregnant women, and over 180 UK organisations now believe that children should be protected from all forms of physical punishment (Children are Unbeatable! 1998).

UK implementation of the Convention on the Rights of the Child

In 1999 the Government will present its second report on implementation of the UN Convention on the Rights of the Child to the Committee on the Rights of the Child. The Committee is the internationally-elected human rights Treaty Body established by the Convention to monitor its implementation worldwide.

Article 3 of the Convention states that the best interests of the child shall be a primary consideration in all actions concerning children, and Article 19 states that governments which ratify the Convention:

> *'... shall take all appropriate legislative, administrative, social and educational measures to protect the child from all forms of physical or mental violence, injury or abuse, neglect or negligent treatment, maltreatment or exploitation, including sexual abuse, while in the care of parent(s), legal guardian(s) or any other person who has the care of the child.*
>
> *Such protective measures should, as appropriate, include effective procedures for the establishment of social programmes to provide necessary support for the child and for those who have the care of the child ...'*

When it examined the UK's first report, in 1995, among the Committee's concerns was the law allowing 'reasonable chastisement'. The Committee stated it was *'worried about the national legal provisions dealing with reasonable chastisement within the family. The imprecise nature of the expression of reasonable chastisement as contained in these legal provisions may pave the way for it to be interpreted in a subjective and arbitrary manner...The Committee recommends that physical punishment of children in families be prohibited...[and] the Committee suggests that the State Party consider the possibility of undertaking additional education campaigns. Such measures would help to change societal attitudes towards the use of physical punishment in the family and foster the acceptance of the legal prohibition of the physical punishment of children'.*

The UK has not been singled out for criticism: the Committee has consistently held that physical punishment of children is not compatible with the principles and provisions of the Convention, and has recommended prohibition and educational initiatives to promote non-violent discipline. In its follow-up report to the Committee the Government will be expected to set out what action it has taken as a result of the Committee's formal recommendations. The Committee's guidelines for periodic reports asks: 'whether legislation (criminal and/or family law) includes a prohibition of all forms of physical and mental violence, including corporal punishment, deliberate humiliation, injury, abuse, neglect or exploitation, *inter alia* within the family, in foster and other forms of care, and in public or private institutions, such as penal institutions and schools'.

The Committee also recommended that the UK should end corporal punishment in private schools. Here there has been progress: the Government's School Standards and Framework Act 1998 includes a provision which removes the defence of 'reasonable chastisement' altogether in relation to punishment of children in schools and nurseries, thereby giving them the same protection as adults under the law on assault.

The law which allows corporal punishment of children

Children are the only people in the UK who can still legally be hit. Parents and other carers have a common law freedom to use 'reasonable chastisement'. The still-quoted leading case dates back to 1860. In it, Chief Justice Cockburn stated: *'By the law of England, a parent ... may for the purpose of correcting what is evil in the child, inflict moderate and reasonable corporal punishment, always, however, with this condition, that it is moderate and reasonable'.* (The common law is confirmed in England and Wales in the Children and Young Persons Act 1933 and in similar statutes applying in Scotland and Northern Ireland).

It is interesting to note that when children first received limited protection from parents in the Prevention of Cruelty to and Protection of Children Act 1889 this came 66 years after similar legislation was passed protecting animals.

In recent years judges and juries in UK courts have acquitted parents who admitted to beating their children with belts, sticks and electric flexes, causing bruising and other injuries, and successfully used the 'reasonable chastisement' defence to justify their actions.

Outside the home, the law has moved slowly to protect children from corporal punishment. Children are recorded as presenting a petition to Parliament in 1669 (Newell, 1989, p131) protesting against school corporal punishment. Yet it has taken more than three centuries for Parliament to respond by prohibiting all corporal punishment in schools. Forced to act by a series of decisions of the European Human Rights Commission and Court in the 1980s, corporal punishment was ended in all state-supported education in the UK by legislation which came into force in 1987. The right to use it lingered on in the private sector. Then, this year, both Houses of Parliament accepted a provision which extends the ban to cover all schools and nursery education.

Regulations introduced in 1991 prohibit corporal punishment in residential children's homes and in foster care arranged by local authorities or voluntary organisations. Guidance issued under the Children Act 1989 discourages corporal punishment in private foster care and in day care. But in March 1994 a High Court judge upheld a childminder's application to be allowed to smack children in her care with their parents' permission, and subsequently the Department of Health issued a circular (LAC (94) 23) condoning the use of a 'gentle smack' by childminders with parents' consent.

Prevalence of physical punishment of children in the UK

Research shows that most young children, including babies, in the UK are hit by their parents.

Marjorie Smith and colleagues at the Thomas Coram Research Unit recently completed comprehensive research, funded by the Department of Health, on the prevalence of violence in the home and children's views of appropriate parental punishment (1995). They interviewed over 500 mothers of children aged one, four, seven or eleven years and concluded that the large majority of children experience some form of physical punishment in the home. The sample was drawn from child health registers in two different areas in the UK. They found that:

- almost three-quarters of children were hit within the last year[1];
- 29% of children had been physically restrained in the last year[2];
- almost 14% of children had been punished by example[3];
- 5% of children had experienced forced ingestion[4].

The large majority of severe incidents (15 % of sample) related to hitting. Over three-quarters of mothers with one-year-old babies admitted to hitting them in the previous year[5]. Over a third of these mothers said they had hit their babies more than once in the previous week.

---

1   This included hitting, cuffing, tapping, smacking, slapping, spanking, thumping, punching, beating, kicking and throwing objects.

2   This included wiping face with cold flannel, physically restraining child, cold bath/shower, hand/object over mouth, placing head under water, shaking, pushing/shoving and throwing.

3   This category related to parental actions based on trying to show children the consequences of their actions and included pulling hair, scratching, pinching, biting/nipping/chewing, burning and putting in cold water.

4   This included being forced to eat food, made to eat something nasty (eg mustard sandwiches), forced to drink salt water, washing mouth out with soap and water, forced to drink poisonous or dangerous substances.

5   Mothers, while admitting to hitting when asked by researchers, were then asked what word they used to describe their actions. Many used the word 'tapping'.

Usually prevalence studies focus on one parent alone, questioning how much they hit or physically punish children. A more 'child-centred' approach seeks to find out how much children are hit. When Nobes and Smith (1997) uniquely interviewed both parents in 99 two-parent families, they uncovered the huge under-reporting of previous studies.

(See box overleaf.)

How much are children hit?

A recent study, funded by the Department of Health, interviewed both parents in 99 families, and revealed that (Nobes and Smith, 1997):

- 52% of one-year-olds were hit/smacked at least once a week by their parents; 12% (three infants) were reported to be hit or smacked daily or more often by a parent.
- 48% of four-year-olds were hit/smacked at least once a week by their parents.
- 35% of seven-year-olds were hit/smacked at least once a week by their parents.
- 11% of 11-year-olds were hit/smacked at least once a week by their parents.
- More than a fifth of mothers and fathers had inflicted 'severe' punishments on children.
- Implements (usually slippers or wooden spoons) were used by 14% of mothers and 15% of fathers.
- Over 90% of mothers and fathers reported physically punishing their children at some time.
- Over 80% of mothers and fathers had physically punished children in the previous year.
- The most common form of physical punishment for both mothers and fathers was hitting/smacking, which had been used by 94% of mothers and 91% of fathers.

Nobes and Smith (1997, p279) concluded that *'the data show that children in two-parent families are physically punished considerably more than they are punished either by mothers or by fathers alone. Estimates based on the reports of only one parent in each family will, therefore, lead to serious underestimation of the true extent of physical punishment to children'.*

Previous longitudinal research carried out by John and Elizabeth Newson (1989) in 1958 through to the 1970s on 700 families in Nottingham reported that:
- 62% of one-year-olds had been smacked;
- 97% of four-year-olds had been smacked;
- 22% of seven-year-olds had been hit with an implement (professional parents were found to be most likely to use implements).

Adults' attitudes towards physical punishment in the UK

In 1994 the NSPCC commissioned Research Surveys of Great Britain (RSGB) to carry out a survey of adults' childhood experiences, linking these with their current attitudes towards child-rearing. Over 1000 people aged between 18 and 45 years across England, Scotland and Wales were interviewed using two questionnaires (Creighton and Russell, 1995). As part of the wider survey, participants were asked to state whether they agreed or disagreed with a set of statements about child-rearing and promoting positive behaviour among children. This is a selection of some of the findings:

	% agree	% disagree
Showing you care for them is a good way of ensuring children try to behave as you would wish.	95	2
The way to deal with a child who misbehaves is to try to reason with them and show them how their actions hurt other people.	94	2
If you show respect to a child it is more likely to grow up into a responsible adult.	91	4
A good slap does no real harm if a child is misbehaving.	70	20
It's the right of parents to punish a child however they see fit without anyone else interfering.	66	26

We can see that, although 95% of respondents thought that showing children you care for them is a good way of encouraging positive behaviour, 70% believed 'a good slap does no real harm'. 66 % of the sample believed that parents should be able to do anything they like to punish children without any outside interference.

These alarming findings suggest that many adults continue to believe that it is adults' prerogative to decide acceptable limits of punishment. While the law encourages and supports the view that parents can exercise total discretion on how to discipline children, attitudes like these will be hard to shift. Again we can draw hope from other countries where smacking has been outlawed: research in Sweden shows that since children gained legal protection from all forms of assault in 1978 attitudes among both adults and children have shifted dramatically in favour of non-violent forms of discipline (Hakansson, 1996).

Children's attitudes towards parental physical punishment

When Smith and her colleagues (1995) interviewed 205 children, aged seven and 11 years, they found that younger children and boys were more likely to suggest physical punishment as being the likely parental response to various actions by children such as stealing, lying, disobedience, aggression to siblings and danger to self. Using vignettes illustrated with pictures or drawings, they asked children to describe what parents would do in particular situations. They found that seven-year-olds who are subject to more serious physical punishment are more likely to suggest smacking as a parental response to dealing with various situations; this association subsided to the point where it was not evident in the 11-year-old children.

This research suggests that young children's attitudes towards physical punishment are affected by their own experience of being hit: the more children are hit they more they expect others to be hit. It would have been useful if Smith and others had consistently asked children whether they thought adults *should* hit as this would have explored their own individual attitudes rather than simply requiring them to predict adult behaviour. Nevertheless, this study raises important lessons for working towards a non-violent society – clearly the more children experience violence, the more legitimate violence becomes.

A MORI survey, conducted for the NSPCC, of 998 eight to 15-year-olds growing up in the 1990s (Ghate and Daniels, 1997) included a section on children's attitudes towards the effectiveness of various methods of parental discipline. The most frequently mentioned method was rational explanation, with 61% of the total sample believing that 'talking to you and explaining why what you did was wrong' was most effective. There was a significant age difference: 52% of eight to 11-year-olds compared to 70% of 12 to 15-year-olds favoured reasoning. Only 11% of children believed that slapping or smacking was an effective method of stopping a child their age behaving badly in future. Again there was a noticeable age split: 15% of eight to 11-year-olds compared to 7% of 12 to 15-year-olds said smacking was effective.

These differences in age are likely to reflect children's direct experiences, with younger children possibly encountering less rational discussion with parents but having more current experience of being slapped or smacked.

The smacking debate: missing voices

We are not aware of any study or consultation exercise which has comprehensively sought the direct views of young children on smacking. Indeed we have been unable to trace *any* examples of children of whatever age being asked in a straightforward way to define smacking, to say what it feels like to be smacked, and to make suggestions about what can be done to prevent smacking.

Article 12 of the UN Convention on the Rights of the Child states that children have a right to express their views in all matters which affect them, giving due weight to their age and maturity. NCB and Save the Children have been listening closely to young children for many decades and we know that they are able to consider difficult issues and come up with solutions and ideas that older people often miss. Only children can speak from direct, contemporary experience of being smacked; only they can tell us what it *really* feels like to be smacked, and only they can tell us whether, from a child's perspective, smacking is an effective part of helping children be caring and responsible citizens, now and in the future.

Why consult young children?

The National Children's Bureau and Save the Children set out to interview young children – five, six and seven-year-olds – about smacking for two reasons. First, because we fully support the right of children to express their views in all matters which affect them, as laid down in Article 12 of the UN Convention on the Rights of the Child. Second, because we know from research that physical punishment is mostly directed at young children (Newson and Newson, 1989; Smith, 1995).

A commitment to the human rights of children

Both organisations are committed to full implementation of the UN Convention on the Rights of the Child. Among the fundamental principles of human rights are respect for human dignity and physical integrity and equality before the law. While the physical punishment of children – smacking, slapping, pinching, beating – remains socially and legally acceptable, the UK clearly breaches these principles, and persists in supporting traditional attitudes to children as possessions rather than individual people. We therefore believe, in common with over 180 organisations working with or for children, that children should have the same protection as adults under the law on assault and that concepts such as 'reasonable chastisement' should be consigned to history, along with the 'rule of thumb' that used to determine the thickness of a stick with which a husband was deemed to have the right to beat his wife.

An anti-family project?

Some may criticise us for asking children such questions at all, suggesting the exercise is 'anti-family', or undermining proper respect for parental authority. First, we emphasise that no child was interviewed without the full and informed consent of his or her parents or carers. Second, we believe the responses overwhelmingly demonstrate that respect between children and parents will be hugely enhanced once smacking is rejected and replaced with positive, non-violent forms of discipline.

There is no sense in which promoting the principles in the Convention on the Rights of the Child is anti-family. On the contrary, the Convention is passionately supportive of the family, which it describes as '... the fundamental group of society and the natural environment for the growth and well-being of all its members and particularly children'. The Convention requires the state to respect the rights and responsibilities of parents; to support the family in a variety of ways; to keep families together and re-unite families and only separate children in extreme circumstances in the best interests of the child; and to promote the child's respect for his or her parents as an aim of education.

But where will all this lead?

Finally, one other misconception is that removing the defence of 'reasonable chastisement' to give children equal protection under the law on assault will lead to more prosecutions of parents, and inappropriate state intervention in the family. Trivial assaults of adults do not reach court, and nor would trivial assaults of children. We know from the experience of other countries that law reform coupled with promotion of positive ways of disciplining children rapidly changes attitudes and reduces reliance on physical punishment: this will reduce the need for prosecutions and child protection interventions.

5. Method of consultation

Getting started

The purpose of this consultation exercise was to give young children – aged five to seven years – the opportunity to express their views about smacking, which could then be fed into the Government's wider consultation on physical punishment. 76 children took part; another eight participated in an initial pilot. Contact with children was gained through sending a project description to 70 primary schools which are members of the National Children's Bureau inviting them to take part; and to schools and organisations who have worked with Save the Children.

The pilot interview was conducted in a school already known to the project workers. The remaining group discussions were carried out in six primary schools and two play schemes. Five were state schools (one Church of England), and one was independent. The state schools were reported to have a varied intake of children from socially diverse catchment areas. The two summer play schemes were run by a North London local authority.

Once schools or organisations expressed an interest information sheets were sent for distribution to parents/carers of all children in the relevant age group (five to seven-year-olds). The information sheet asked parents to give written permission for their children to take part in a small group discussion where children would be asked to:

- describe what a smack is;
- say how children feel when they are smacked;
- explain why, when and where children are smacked;
- give advice on what could be done to reduce or stop smacking.

It was made clear to parents/carers that the project did not aim to encourage children to talk in detail about their own experiences. The letter clearly stated that the intention was to encourage children to give general information and advice to the project workers.

Parents were also told that if a child did want to talk about any personal experiences, either during or after the group discussion, then the school/centre would follow normal procedures.

The process

Sixteen group discussions were held with between three and six children during July and August 1998. In 14 of the 16 groups children were split according to age so we listened to five, six and seven-year-olds separately. Before starting each discussion the purpose of the project was described, and we explained our organisations' intention to publish our findings to ensure Tony Blair and other members of the Government would hear their views (see section 10 'Lessons in Listening'). Children were given the opportunity to opt out of taking part before the discussions began.

Discussions were held using a specially commissioned story book featuring a green character called Splodge. During the course of the project this character was variously described as an alien, a brain, a fruit, a monster and a frog by the children who took part. Splodge was introduced to children as being very curious about life on earth, especially about smacking. Splodge asked children the following questions:

Splodge's questions:

- **Who knows what a smack is?**
- **Why do you think children get smacked?**
- **Who usually smacks children?**
- **Where do children usually get smacked?**
- **What does it feel like to be smacked?**
- **How do children act after being smacked? How do adults act after they have given a smack?**
- **Adults smack children but why don't children smack adults? Children smack each other but why don't adults smack each other?**
- **When you are big do you think you will smack children?**
- **Do you know anybody who doesn't like smacking? Who thinks it is wrong to smack?**
- **How can we stop children being smacked?**

Discussions varied in length between 30 minutes to over an hour depending on how many children were involved, and how much they had to contribute. Each child was encouraged to answer each question; on a few occasions individual children declined to answer a particular question.

The two project workers took turns to lead discussions and take notes. The discussions were also tape-recorded and transcribed to ensure none of the children's contributions were lost. In 14 of the 16 discussions, school or play scheme staff were present throughout. Although they took no part in the process, their presence was invaluable as they undoubtedly helped children to trust us.

At the end of each discussion, children were asked to complete a form which recorded their age, ethnic origin, who they lived with and whether they had any special educational needs.

From the 76 children who took part only four children in one group of five-year-olds did not complete their group discussion.

Each of the schools and play schemes which took part were given book or toy vouchers to thank them for their help.

6. Children who took part in group discussions

As can be seen from tables 6.1 to 6.7, the sample comprised slightly more girls (57%) than boys (43%). Of the children who took part 32% were aged 5 years, 32% 6 years and 36% were aged 7 years. One child was 4 years old.

Almost 80 % of the children who took part were white; 20% were from black and minority ethnic groups. Black and minority ethnic groups comprise approximately 5% of the general population in the UK, although there is a higher percentage of children from black and minority communities under the age of 16 than in the rest of the population.

We found in the pilot group discussion that children did not understand what we meant by 'disabled' or 'special educational needs' so the term 'special help' was used instead to record this information. 18% of the children said they needed special help in school; this ranged from having a classroom assistant, to needing help with reading or maths.

Fifty per cent of those who took part live in the South of England while 26% live in the Midlands and 24% in the North of England.

The majority (72%) of the children were living with both birth parents. Over half of them (51%) also lived with siblings.

6.1 Sex	No.	%
Female	43	57
Male	33	43
Total	**76**	**100**

6.2 Age	No.	%
4 years	1	1
5 years	24	32
6 years	24	32
7 years	27	36
Total	**76**	**100**

6.3 Ethnic origin

	No.	%
Black	4	5
Chinese	1	1
Egyptian	1	1
Indian	1	1
Irish	1	1
Mixed	7	9
Turkish	1	1
White	60	79
Total	**76**	**98**

6.4 Special help

	No.	%
Yes	14	18
No	62	82
Total	**76**	**100**

6.6 Where they live

	No.	%
South	38	50
Midlands	20	26
North	18	24
Total	**76**	**100**

6.7 Who they live with

	No.	%
Both birth parents and siblings	39	51
Both birth parents – no siblings	16	21
Lone parent – no siblings	7	9
Lone parent and siblings	5	7
Birth parent and partner and siblings	3	4
Both birth parents, siblings and another adult	2	3
Both birth parents and another adult	1	1
Birth parent and partner	1	1
Lone parent, siblings and adult relative	1	1
Foster mother	1	1
Total	**76**	**99**

7. Children's messages to adults

This section communicates children's direct experiences, thoughts and views on smacking. Each question is taken in turn with a summary in table form of what children said, a short interpretation followed by a broad selection of direct quotes from the children.

The tables present the frequency of particular answers from different children. The responses from children to each question often gave us a wealth of information rather than single word answers. For example, when we asked *who usually smacks children* invariably each child gave us a list of different people. Some questions – such as *who thinks it's wrong to smack* – were more straightforward to record. Repetitions of the same point from a child were not counted. Finally, at the end of each section we have included a shaded box depicting key themes and discussion points.

Careful consideration was given on how to present the diversity and range of children's responses in a clear and accessible way. The aim was to ensure the reader had access to the richness of information, while avoiding an over-reliance on lists or general comments which fail to sum up adequately how often children gave similar responses. The tables are to be interpreted broadly as indicating common themes and responses. The purpose of giving all children the opportunity to answer all questions was to give them space to share their individual insights, experiences and opinions. In this respect, a comment made by only one or two children is as equally valid and important as points raised by many.

If a child repeated the same answer it was counted only once in the relevant category. Obviously many children gave answers that could be included in more than one category. For instance, when asked 'Do you know anybody who doesn't like smacking?' (Q9a) one five-year-old boy answered, 'myself, my dad, my mum, my sister'. This answer was counted in each category of 'me', 'dad', 'mum', 'brothers and sisters'. In most cases, therefore, the total number of responses in a table will add up to more than 76 as children's statements were broken down and included in more than one category.

The alternative to using tables would have been to supply the reader with information such as 'many children said', 'some said' or 'a few children noted that'. We believe this would not have done justice to this particular project, although we recognise the difficulties our chosen method may present.

All names have been changed so that individual children, schools or play schemes cannot be identified. Quotes have been separated according to themes and, wherever possible, the sex and age of the children has been included.

Q1. Who knows what a smack is?

Children's definition of a smack	Frequency (no. of different children who gave this answer)
It's a hard hit	17
It's a hit	15
A very hard hit/a hard, hard hit/a big hard hit	11
It hurts/it really hurts/it makes you feel hurt	11
It happens when you're naughty/bad	10
It's when you poke/whack/hit/slap/fight/hurt	10
It gives you a rash/it itches/stings/burns	4
It happens when people are cross	4
It isn't very nice/it's a bad thing to do	4
It makes you/someone cry	3
It's like a pat only harder	1
It's like clapping	1

The message from children is that a smack is a hit: on 43 occasions children described a smack as a hit, a hard hit or a very hard hit. A five-year-old girl explained that a smack is *'when someone hits you really hard'*, a seven-year-old girl said a smack is *'a big hard hit'* while a six-year-old boy said *'it's when you get hit'*. A seven-year-old boy told us *'my dad's hard at smacking, very hard'* while a six-year-old confirmed her view that smacking cannot be soft or gentle:

Child *It's a really hard hit*
Adult Can it be a soft hit?
Child *No*

Only one child described a smack as a 'pat' quickly adding that it is 'only harder'.

Children described the impact of being hit, and said that it hurts:

It's like very hard hitting and it hurts you' (six-year-old girl)
'Something what hurts people...grown ups hit you with their hand – it's something hard' (seven-year-old girl)
'It really hurts' (five-year-old girl)
'A smack is when people hit you and it stings and I cry' (five-year-old girl)

Children being naughty or bad is mentioned in responses from 10 children in the older age groups: *'when people do something naughty they get smacked'* (six-year-old boy), and *'when you be bad, you get a smack'* (six-year-old boy). Being naughty was not mentioned by the five-year-olds at all.

A small number of children said that a smack is given when people are cross:

> *'Well, it's usually when someone is cross with you. They smack you to try and stop you from doing it'* (six-year-old girl)
> *'It's when someone is cross with you they hit you and it hurts'* (seven-year-old girl)

Children did not only answer this question in words; frequently they stood up to give us or Splodge a demonstration of what a smack is. We witnessed children energetically swinging their hands towards their legs, bottoms and arms to hit themselves with varying degrees of force. On some occasions they gave a demonstration then informed us a 'real smack' would be a lot harder. A seven-year-old girl observed:

> *'[A smack is] parents trying to hit you, [but] instead of calling [it] a hit they call it a smack'*

Responses were sometimes ambiguous and the group setting meant we were not always able to clarify points in detail. For instance, a five-year-old girl said *'It's when you hit your hand on people hard'*. Is she talking about herself as someone who smacks, or is she telling us about how people generally smack? Children answered the question from varying perspectives; sometimes in the first person drawing directly on their own experiences and other times in the third person. From these answers we get a sense of children's perceptions of smacking as well as their experiences.

Who knows what a smack is?
A selection of quotes from children

Who knows what a 'smack' is?

It's a hard hit/a hit

'I think it's just something parents sort of do [they] hit you... it's not really a punch or anything it's just really a hit' (seven-year-old girl)

'When you're naughty – a grown up comes along – [it's] hardish' (six-year-old)

'It's when you hit your hand on people hard' (five-year-old girl)

'It's when you hit someone in the face' (five-year-old boy)
'Your mums and dads hit you when you've been naughty' (six-year-old girl)
'It's where you hit somebody somewhere' (six-year-old girl)
'Hitting like that [shows by slapping arm] like you're fighting with someone' (five-year-old girl)
'Well, it's something where somebody hits you with their hand open like that' Does it make a sound?
'Sometimes' (seven-year-old boy)
'It's when something hits you' (seven-year-old girl)
'[It's when] someone who like hits someone' (seven-year-old girl)
'Uh, well [it's] when somebody hits you hard' (six-year-old girl)
'It's a really hard hit' Can it be a soft hit? *'No'* (six-year-old girl)
'It's really hard [shows action]' (six-year-old)
'It's when you get slapped hard' (five-year-old girl)

A very hard hit/a hard, hard hit/ a big hard hit

> *'It's when someone smacks you really hard'* (five-year-old girl)

'It's when you hit someone very hard' (five-year-old boy)
'It's when someone hits you really hard' (five- year-old)
'You have to do it really hard' (six-year-old boy)
'It's when you've been naughty and you get a smack, a very hard one' (seven-year-old girl)

It hurts/it really hurts/ it makes you feel hurt

> *'A smack is if someone hurts you on accident or on purpose'* (six-year-old boy)

'It's something when you hurt somebody like slapping' (five-year-old girl)
'It's this [demonstrates], ow, I hurt my hand' (five-year-old boy)

It happens when you are naughty or bad

'When people do something naughty they get smacked' (six-year-old boy)
'[You get smacked] when you're dead naughty – when you swear' (six-year-old girl)
'It's what you get when you've been naughty' (six-year-old girl)
'It's what someone [would] do if someone's been naughty – it hurts' (seven-year-old boy)

It's when you poke, whack, hit, slap or fight someone

'It's when you whack somebody in the head' (five-year-old boy)
'It's when you kick somebody' (five-year old)
'Like it's just like slapping people but it has a different name' (five-year-old)
'It's when you hit someone' (six-year-old girl)

It gives you a rash; it itches, stings or burns

'If someone's naughty or something and you smack them just here it hurts and [it] gives you a rash round here' (seven-year-old boy)

It isn't very nice; it's a bad thing to do

'Smacking is a very bad thing to do' (five-year-old girl)
'A smack is not very nice, and if you're naughty to your mum, your mum and dad smack you back. Say you're being naughty to your mum and your dad's at work, yeh, your dad comes home, yeh, and your mum tells your dad how much you've been naughty and your dad will give you a big smack' (seven-year-old boy)
'[It's] something what isn't very nice' (seven-year-old girl)

It makes you cry

'It makes you cry' (six-year-old boy)
'When Daddies or Mummies smack little children cry' (six-year-old girl)

Q2. Why do children usually get smacked?

Reason children get smacked	Frequency (no. of different children who gave this answer)
Being violent or nasty themselves	49
Being naughty or mischievous	41
Breaking or spoiling things	24
Not listening to or disobeying parents	13
Being cheeky/rude/screaming	8
Touching things when they have been told not to/ touching dangerous things	6
Taking things without asking or stealing	6
Swearing	6
Annoying their parents	5
Not tidying up	5
Going off somewhere without parents' permission	3
Because they hit their parents	3
Throwing stones	2
Because parents are cross	2
Not eating/wasting/playing with food	2
It's horrible/it happens in horrible families	2
Because they talked to strangers	1
Because they are jealous	1

There were full and varied answers to this question. Being naughty was mentioned by a large number of children. When asked to describe the sort of things that were naughty, we were given 49 examples of hurting others through fighting, pushing, punching and pulling hair, and 24 examples of breaking or spoiling things.

From children's perspective, it seems that one of the main reasons adults smack is because children themselves have been violent:

Child   *When I'm very naughty my mum smacks me*
Adult   What is being very naughty?
Child   *When you hit people a lot* (five-year-old girl)

'When people have been naughty and they're fighting they get smacked by [their] mum or dad' (six-year-old boy)
'[Being naughty is] hitting people [and] pushing people over' (five-year-old boy)
'[Children get smacked] when you fight with other people, when you throw stones and things' (seven-year-old boy)

Over 20 examples of breaking or spoiling things were given as reasons for children getting smacked. A typical example of the sorts of things that might warrant a smack were given by this five-year-old girl:

'Maybe [you] do painting on the carpet [or] drawing on the settee [or] not tidying your room up – if you play with paint and get it on something. And if you knock your mum's favourite glass over and it smashes'

Other examples include ripping and drawing on books, spilling something over on purpose, breaking things in the house, and writing on walls.

Not listening to or disobeying parents were given as reasons for being smacked. For instance, *'well, if it was time to tidy up your room and you only had an hour and you wasted all the hour reading books, you could get smacked'* (six-year-old boy) or more simply, *'because their parents tell them not to do something and they do it'* (seven-year-old girl).

Being rude to parents by, for example, *'sticking your tongue out'* (seven-year-old girl) or *'being cheeky to grown ups'* (six-year-old girl) were given as reasons by some children.

Children also mentioned swearing as being the cause of a smack: *'I think they get smacked because they're naughty [and they] like say the 'f word'* (seven-year-old girl) or *'all the mams get mad when you swear'* (seven-year-old girl).

Touching things that they have been told not to touch such as 'mum's things' or cookers and light bulbs were mentioned by three different children.

Interestingly only one seven-year-old boy mentioned smacking as a way of deterring children from doing something dangerous, which he then mentioned several times, *'say if your mum was to go out yeh for about three minutes yeh and if you touched the cooker or hot stuff then your mum and dad comes in and find out, they'll go mad with you'*.

Some children said smacking could happen if children take or steal things: *'if you take a sweet without asking'* (six-year-old girl).

A seven-year-old girl gave a rare answer to this question, implying that adults sometimes use smacking as a considered response to children's behaviour:

'Well mummy always says to me that children only would get smacked if there is not another way and they have done something really naughty'

Two of the younger children told us that *'it's not very nice to smack, it's horrible'* and *'some people have horrible families and they get smacked when they've been naughty'*.

Why do children usually get smacked: key themes and discussion points

Children said that children are smacked because they have been naughty. When asked to describe what kinds of things are naughty, many examples were given: being violent or nasty to others; breaking and spoiling things; and disobeying and not listening to parents.

It is noticeable that the primary reason this group of children think children get smacked is because they have hurt others. This is a powerful message – that it is not OK for them to hurt others but it is OK for a larger person to hurt them. It is interesting to consider the impact of this contradictory message on children: a child is told that it is wrong to hurt someone and then is hurt in response.

Many of the examples of being naughty clearly warrant a response from parents, but is smacking the most appropriate way of discouraging violence in young children?

The majority of children in all groups talked about smacking in relation to adults smacking children, although smacking between children was mentioned.

Why do children usually get smacked?
A selection of quotes from children

Being violent or nasty themselves

Why do you think children get smacked?

'Because you hit your friend and then they go and tell your mother then your mum comes along and smacks you' (six-year-old boy)

'Because they've been very naughty – when they smack other children' (five-year-old girl)

'Because they're naughty – if they're smacking other people' (five-year-old boy)
'When they get caught pulling hair' (five-year-old boy)
'Because sometimes other people hurt them and they hurt them back' (five-year-old girl)
'Sometimes when they smack the other child and the child smacks them back and then they smack him back then the other one tells the teacher' (five-year-old girl)
'When they be naughty. When you push them over. When you chuck something at them. When you whack them in the eye [or] when you punch them in the leg' (five-year-old boy)
'When people hit...then your mummy or dad – they're not supposed to – they smack you' (five-year-old girl)
'Because they're very naughty' What kind of things are naughty? 'Throwing stones' (five-year-old boy)
'Because sometimes they kick somebody, or they go into somebody's house without asking their mum' Any other reasons? 'Biting' (six-year-old girl)

'When you be naughty...and like, if you be fighting with your brother or sister...then they might tell mum to smack you' (six-year-old boy)

'They might be naughty' What kind of things are naughty? *'Like if they spit on someone or if they fight at school [or] if they go off with somebody else'* (six-year-old boy)

'Pulling hair' (six-year-old girl)

'For being horrid to their sister' (six-year-old girl)

'Because they have been naughty and maybe hit their younger or older sister or just got their parents so annoyed that they don't know what to do with them so they just smack' (seven-year-old girl)

'Because they're naughty' What kind of things are naughty? *'Hurting people [and] spilling something over on purpose'* (seven-year-old girl)

'Because you've hit mum or dad and then they hit you back' (seven-year-old girl)

'Because they're naughty' What kind of things do children do? *'Write all over the walls [and] kick their mums if they've got bad legs'* (seven-year-old girl)

Breaking or spoiling things

'Being naughty by breaking or spoiling things – because they're mischievous' What kind of things do they do if they're mischievous? *'They mess up their room and don't tidy it back and they bite their teddies...and they push people over'* (five-year-old girl)

'Because they are naughty. Smash cars ... smash car windows' (five-year-old girl)

'He might rip a book and get smacked' Anything else? *'He might write in something that he's not supposed to write'* What like? *'Swear words'* (seven-year-old boy)

'I think they get smacked because they have done something naughty' Could you give any examples? *'Well like people falling down the chair [or] they could knock the clock or mirror, and they could knock their mirrors and they could push'* (seven-year-old boy)

'If your parents told you not to swing on a gate and you break it' (seven-year-old boy)

> **'Because their parents tell them not to do things and they do it'** (seven-year-old girl)

Not listening to or disobeying parents

'Well, if it was time to tidy up your room and you only had an hour and you wasted all the hour reading books, you could get smacked' (six-year-old boy)

'When you've been playing with your bike and she tells you to go and put it in the garden and you don't' (six-year-old girl)

'Because their parents don't want them to do something' (six-year-old girl)

'Because if they're naughty and they won't, if their mum says go to your room and you don't and keep on saying that and he still doesn't – but if he does as he's told be won't get smacked' (seven-year-old)

'Play with people you're not meant to play with cos they're being nasty to you and you're not allowed to play with them anymore' (seven-year-old boy)

> **'Because they're not listening to their mums or not putting their books away or they're not eating their food or they're wasting it'** (five-year-old girl)

Swearing

'Cause they're always being naughty' What kind of things to they do? *'They swear and they always hit'* Who do they hit? *'Grown ups'* (six-year-old boy)

'Cause when they are being naughty' What kind of things do they do? *'Pulling hair, being cheeky to grown ups [and] when you swear at your mum'* (six-year-old girl)

Touching things they're not supposed to

> *'Taking things without asking or stealing. If you take a sweet without asking you might get a smack for doing that'* (six-year-old girl)

'If your dad's a workman and he keeps his van in the drive and you play in it, you might get smacked' You might get smacked? *'Because he might get fed up with you there, with big tools or something'* (six-year-old boy)
'If you touch the light in your bedroom and you touch the light when its still on and you burn your finger off and you have to be honest' (seven-year-old boy)

Taking things or stealing

'Because they are naughty and their parents get mad' What kind of things are naughty? *'Spilling things [and] taking things that they're not supposed to, like money'* (seven-year-old girl)

Not tidying up

'When you be naughty and you get a smack and you like – if you don't tidy your bedroom sometimes you might get a smack as well' (seven-year-old girl)

Annoying parents

'Annoying their parents – because they're naughty' Because they're naughty? *'They annoy their parents, they go into their parents' bedroom and they're not allowed [and] when they get grounded they go outside'* (seven-year-old boy)

Being cheeky or rude

'When they've been very naughty' What kind of things are naughty? *'Being rude like sticking your tongue out to other people'* (boy)
'A smack is when children get smacked because sometimes they be naughty like sometimes I be naughty and I get smacked' What kinds of things do children do when they're naughty? *'They fight at home – they probably be rude to their mother'* (six-year-old boy)

Throwing stones

'You could like throw stones at someone and then your friend goes to your door and knocks on it then your mum comes out and then says 'what's up?'. And then they say that you've been throwing stones at them and then your mum could give you a smack' (six-year-old boy)

Because parents are cross

'Their parents usually get cross and erm they just go really over the top' (seven-year-old girl)

Not eating or wasting/playing with food

'Because they've been naughty' What kind of things are naughty? *'Play about with their food [or] ripping books [or] writing in books that you're not allowed to [and] playing about with things that you're not allowed to'* (seven-year-old girl)

Because they talked to strangers

'When they talk to strangers' (seven-year-old girl)

Q3. Who usually smacks children?

Who usually smacks children	Frequency (no. of different children who gave this answer)
Mums	43
Dads	40
Grannies	30
Grandads	24
A grown up	13
Brothers	13
Children	12
Sisters	11
Aunties	10
Parents	6
Uncles	6
Cousins	5
Grandparents	4
Nannies (carers)	4
Strangers/nasty men	4
Anybody/people	3
Policemen	3
Friends	2
Teachers	2
Bullies	2
Teenagers	2
Foster people	1
Children of foster carers	1
Baby sitters	1

Parents were mentioned by all the children who answered this question. Mums were mentioned 43 times while dads were referred to on 40 occasions. Children listed a number of other people in children's lives who smack too, including other children. A six-year-old girl explained:

'Well, I think mostly family and sometimes friends who get quite cross with you like [your] mum and dad, grandma and grandad and friends that live quite near here, in the same street.'

A five-year-old girl gave the following list of people who usually smack children:

'Their parents or your mummy or your daddy or your grandad or your auntie or your grandma or people in your house – a big person has to hit a little person because they're naughty.'

She continued:

'Sometimes if your uncles and aunties are there and your mum and dads are there they can smack you really hard or they can smack you with a cane'

A large number of children gave 'a grown up' as the answer to this question. There was not a noticeable gender difference, although women were mentioned on more occasions than men. This no doubt relates to the fact that women generally spend more time than men with young children.

Some children mentioned adults who are not parents. A seven-year-old girl said *'usually their parents and relations and occasionally you might get a teacher'* while a five-year-old said *'sometimes babysitters'* while another person of the same age proclaimed, *'policemen – my dad's a policeman'*. A six-year-old girl listed *'mums and dads and aunties and foster people and foster children'* while nannies (paid to look after children in the home) were mentioned on four occasions.

There were 58 mentions of grandparents: a seven-year-old girl explained, *'let's say your mum and dad have gone out and you've been naughty, your grandmother [will smack you but] mostly your mum and dad'*.

Children talked about other children smacking too, not just brothers and sisters: *'people in the playground smack children'* (seven-year-old boy), and *'sometimes bullies'* said another seven-year-old boy.

Aunties and uncles were also specifically mentioned: a six-year-old boy said, *'your parents usually smack you and if your auntie is annoyed with you she might smack – or [it can be] any of your family'*.

Strangers and 'nasty men' also presented potential dangers to children. A five-year-old boy listed *'thieves, kidnappers, mums and dads [and] nasty men'* as people who usually smack children.

One child demonstrated that, although smacking was outside her immediate experience, she was able to draw on experience gained elsewhere, through observation of other families perhaps: *'I've never been smacked... your mummy might smack you, your daddy, your brother and granny and grandma and granddaddies'* (five-year-old girl).

Who usually smacks children?
A selection of quotes from children

Who usually smacks children?

Parents

'Let's say your mum and dad have gone out and you've been naughty, your grand-mother [would smack you but] mostly your mum or your dad' (seven-year-old girl)

'Mum and dad, or one of the family [grown ups]' (six-year-old)

'Mummies and daddies' (five-year-old girl)
'Your mum or your dad' (five-year-old boy)
'Only your mum and dad' (five-year-old boy)
'Their parents' (seven-year-old girl)

Many people smack children

'Adults – mums, dads, aunties, grandads and nans' (five-year-old girl)

One of the striking points about responses to this question was the number of people that children described as smacking children – so many children produced lists:

'Big people smack children when they've been mischievous' (five-year-old girl)
'Big people and also grandads, parents or if the children might draw on the curtains or something' (five-year-old girl)
'Adults and nannies and grandmas' (five-year-old girl)
'Mum or dad or nanny or grandpa' (six-year-old)
'Mum or dad, grandad, granny, nanny or cousins' (six-year-old)
'Normally dad, grandpa, granny and sometimes children' (six-year-old)
'Mum and dad, grandma and aunty and uncle' (six-year-old girl)
'Me brother, me sister and me mum and dad' (six-year-old boy)
'Your mum and your dad, and your grandparents' (six-year-old girl)
'Mums and dads, grandads [and] grandmas' (six-year-old boy)

'Grandad, grandma, daddy and mummy [and] sister and brother' (six-year-old boy)

'Grown ups – your mam and your dad, and your nanna and your grandad and...your mum's mum' (six-year-old boy)

'Grown ups – your mam and your dad and your nanna and your grandad' (seven-year-old girl)

'Probably your mum and dad, your grandma and grandad and sometimes your old brothers and sisters' (seven-year-old boy)

'Your cousins, your little baby brothers, and your big brothers, and your big sisters and your mum an dad' (seven-year-old girl)

'Your mums, your daddy and your grandparents as well' (seven-year-old girl)

'Your mum, your dad, your grandma, your grandpa, your uncle or your aunty' (seven-year-old boy)

'Your mum and your dad, your nanna or your grandad' (seven-year-old boy)

Grandparents

'Granny, grandad [and] grandma' (five-year-old boy)

'Your grandparents if they're annoyed with you and your grandma and your grandad' (six-year-old boy)

A grown up

'Some grown ups' (five-year-old)

'Grown ups, and it is usually my mum, aunties and uncles as well' (seven-year-old girl)

'Grown ups' (seven-year-old boy)

'A grown up' (seven-year-old boy)

> **'Sometimes my brother usually smacks and I know how to smack him back'** (seven-year-old boy)

Brothers

'Your brother might' (six-year-old boy)

Aunties

'Your parents usually smack you, and if your auntie is annoyed with you she might smack you or any of your family' (six-year-old)

Sisters

'My sister sometimes smacks me' (five-year-old girl)

Other children

'Sometimes children smack children' (seven-year-old girl)

'Me friends' (seven-year-old girl)

'As Tracy said, people in the playground sometimes smack children – I know one in my class – his name is Robert and sometimes yeh he said 'leave me alone or I'll beat you up' – that's what he said sometimes' (six-year-old boy)

> **'Children normally smack people and your dad normally smacks you'** (five-year-old girl)

Teachers

'Usually their parents and relations and occasionally you might get a teacher' (seven-year-old girl)

Anybody

'It can be anybody' (seven-year-old girl)

Strangers or nasty men

'Strangers [grown ups]' (five-year-old girl)

'Your nanna...your dad... or your mum... or your grandad ...or your nanny...or a man' So who would that be? *'A nasty man who sneaks up when you [are without your] mum or without your daddy'* (five-year-old boy)

Teenagers

'Mum, dad, grandma, grandad, little children, sisters and brothers, teenagers and children from comprehensive schools' (seven-year-old girl)

Babysitters

'Sometimes babysitters' (five-year-old girl)

Bullies

'Mums and Dads or big bullies or children' (five-year-old boy)

Q4. Where do children usually get smacked?

Where do children usually get smacked (location)	Frequency (no. of different children who gave this answer)
At home/in the house	25
In their bedroom	13
When their parents are shopping	9
Living/sitting/front room/lounge	8
Kitchen	8
At their grandparents' house	7
At other relatives' houses	6
School	5
On the street/road	4
In the garden/in the garden shed	4
At the park	2
When they are on holiday/at the beach	2
Upstairs	2
In a car/taxi	2
Mum and dad's bedroom	1
Play room	1
Dining room	1
In the passage/hall	1
In a corner	1
In church	1
When they are watching a football match	1
In the pub	1
In prison	1
At an orphanage	1
Playcentre	1

This question referred to both where on the body children are smacked, and which places or locations children are smacked. We assumed participants would begin answering this question by talking about where on the body children are usually smacked, but almost all of them immediately answered in terms of place. This implies that location carries significance for children.

There were some interesting insights into children's perceptions of how parents think other people view them when they smack. For instance, a six-year-old boy said:

'[Children get smacked] in a corner because the parents wouldn't want to do it so everyone could see cos then [the children] might call someone else and they might come and take the children so they'll go in a corner and smack.'

A seven-year-old boy said children get smacked *'at home or normally where nobody else is'.*

And another seven-year-old boy proffered that,

'If there were thousands of people looking, then [the] mum as well as the child will get very embarrassed probably...it would be a bit rude to do it in front of everybody.'

Another child disagreed, *'well I'm not, I don't exactly think the same as the others. It depends where...you've done it, because sometimes if you were naughty in the street, [the mum] would usually just do it straight away, otherwise they would do it again. So I think wherever you did it, even if there is anyone looking'* (seven-year-old boy).

For other children, parents are not inhibited in public spaces:

'When you go shopping and take something and you go and ask your parents and your parents will hit you and embarrass you' (five-year-old girl)
'Before at Tesco's my mum slapped me round the head at Tesco's but it hurt her and it didn't hurt me' (seven-year-old boy).

On 25 separate occasions children told us that children are smacked in the home; additionally 13 said children are smacked in their bedrooms. Shopping was the next most popular location followed by the lounge or kitchen.

Where do children usually get smacked (on the body)	Frequency (no. of different children who gave this answer)
Bottom/bum	37
Arm	20
Head/face/cheek	19
Hand	18
Leg	12
Back	11
Tummy/belly	9
Thigh	4
On your whole body	3
Toes	2
Hip	2
Knee	1
Shoulder	1

Children said they are usually smacked on the bottom; the bottom or bum was mentioned on 37 separate occasions in response to this particular question. But being smacked on other parts of the body is also commonly described. A five-year-old girl said *'on my bum, on my face, and on my arm and on the belly and on the legs'*. A number of children said that where they get smacked is related to how 'naughty' they are – a seven-year-old explained:

> *'I think children usually get smacked on the side of their face or on their tummy. Sometimes it depends how they were. If they were really naughty, it would be on their bottom but sometimes it's usually on their hands.'*

Given the acknowledged dangers of hitting young children around the head, it was concerning how many referred to head, face or cheek. A seven-year-old gave some important advice:

> *'[To stop smacking] you could write a prescription and send it to your mam and write on what we said and put on very important – don't smack children on the head because you might cause brain damage.'*

Where are children smacked: key themes and discussion points

We encouraged children to give information about both the location and part of the body. We anticipated that children would focus on parts of the body yet much information was given about location. Groups of six and seven-year-olds had interesting discussions about adult reactions to being seen smacking children in public.

Many of the children from all groups talked about smacking as something which predominantly happens in the home.

This question was deliberately ambiguous to enable children to talk about both location and parts of the body. The openness of the question allowed us to make important observations about the importance of location to children in each age group.

Where do children usually get smacked
A selection of quotes from children

Location

At home/in the house
'You might get smacked in the house and you get smacked on your arm' (five-year-old boy)
'In your house' (six-year-old boy)

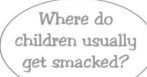

'They might get smacked in the living room or the bedroom or the passage' (five-year-old girl)

Where do children usually get smacked?

It Hurts You Inside

'In the house and at your uncle's house and your cousin's house' (six-year-old boy)

'In the kitchen or living room, in the house [and] in the bedroom' (seven-year-old girl)

'I say at home and the same as everyone else said that children are being naughty and there is no one [there]' (seven-year-old girl)

'At home or normally where nobody else is' Where nobody else is? *'Like somewhere where nobody else is looking'* (seven-year-old boy)

'At home' Is there any particular rooms? *'Living room, bedroom, kitchen and [at] the grandma's house'* Anywhere else? *'Aunties [and] daddies'* (seven-year-old girl)

'In your house or at your grandma's or your grandad's' (seven-year-old boy)

'Anywhere, depends where they are being naughty, if they are being naughty in their sitting room and their mum got very cross with them and then just told them off... and they were naughty again. They kept on doing it then they probably just get smacked somewhere (where) there are not a lot of people, just because it would be rude to do it in front of everybody' Do you think grown ups smack children in private then? *'Yeah, yeah'* Why? *'Because if there were thousands of people looking, then the mum and as well the child will get very embarrassed probably'* (seven-year-old boy)

Bedroom, upstairs or in their parents' bedroom

'You can get smacked in your bedroom because you call your sister and brother a bad word and then you go to your bedroom and then your mummy goes into your bedroom and starts to smack you' (five-year-old girl)

'In the bedroom, [they go] in the bedroom first, then they smack them' (six-year-old boy)

Kitchen

'In the kitchen and in your bedroom' (seven-year-old girl)

Grandparents or other relatives' houses

'At home and at your gran's house or your auntie's house and [at] nannie's [house]'

'At your grandma's, in the lounge, in the kitchen and in your bedroom' (six-year-old girl)

In public

'Maybe at school or in the library or somewhere or maybe at a visitor's house or maybe at the road' (girl)

Shopping

'And when they're shopping they get smacked' (five-year-old boy)

'When you're laughing very loud and your mum's talking to an important person, like a person who gives you the Lottery, you might be laughing so loud your mum could smack you because she won't be able to hear what they're saying' (six-year-old girl)

'When you're at the shop your grandad might smack you' (six-year-old boy)

'When you go shopping and take something and you go and ask your parents and your parents will hit you and embarrass you' (five-year-old girl)

'Sometimes in the shops' Why? *'Because they [children] do things they are not supposed to – they're touching things'* (seven-year-old girl)

'It's usually at home, like Sammy just said, but you might if you were going to the shops and they were climbing around and not paying attention. Whoever was looking after them might get cross and smack them' (seven-year-old girl)

At school or in the playground

'In the playground [and] shopping' (five-year-old boy)

'At school, and on the park' (six-year-old boy)

On the street or road or outside

'When you go to school when you run on the road' (five-year-old girl)

'If they might have been outside and got their clothes all muddy, they might be smacked outside' (six-year-old girl)

'Well when you're outside and you keep crashing your mate's bike yeh, and if your mate knocks on your door, yeh, and they tell of you, your mum might come out and smack you around the head or ear or anywhere else...you know when you're outside yeh and you crash into the wall and then you bust your tyre and your mum gets mad of you and then she smacks you and when my mum smacks me I try not to smack mum. I've only once done it by accident, I wasn't feeling very well and I wasn't thinking that much' (seven-year-old boy)

When they are on holiday or at the beach

'[At] home or in the beach they ran away and their dad find them and smacked them' (five-year-old girl)

'At the beach... then they might swim out to sea and they might get smacked in the playground ... because they've done something naughty' (five-year-old girl)

In other places

'At home and in the garden or maybe when you're going out somewhere' (seven-year-old girl)

'In the car' (five-year-old boy)

'In the church' (seven-year-old girl)

'Watching a football match, on the park [and] in the pub' (seven-year-old boy)

'Well I think they usually get smacked upstairs or [in the] downstairs front room or kitchen [or] if they are shopping if they're getting in the way' (six-year-old girl)

Anywhere – it can be inside or outside

'At home or at school, anywhere' (five-year-old girl)

'Inside and outside' What would happen when it was outside? *'Everybody would tease you'* (five-year-old girl)

'Inside or outside' (six-year-old boy)

'Inside your house or outside' (seven-year-old boy)

'In the living room, in the kitchen, or on the table, in the garden, outside, [and] at home' What do you mean on the table? *'Well, when you are sitting and having lunch and being a bit rude, you get smacked'* (seven-year-old boy)

'Sometimes they get smacked outside or inside' Outside or inside what? *'Might get smacked inside the bedroom and outside because they already got told off, they've been laughing and they might get smacked'* You said you thought children sometimes get smacked outside as well. When does that happen? *'Well, when you've got told off and your mum might say 'don't laugh behind my back' and you laugh behind your mum's back. Then you might get smacked'* (seven-year-old girl)

'Wherever they have been naughty' So where might that be? *'Say you were being naughty in the bedroom. And telling fibs. And if you were being naughty in the hallway, they might smack you in the hallway'* (seven-year-old boy)

On the body

Children get smacked in many different places

'Usually on the hand, on the bum on the arms and sometimes and on the head here [points to side of the head]' (seven-year-old boy)

'Front, leg, and knee and arms and belly, back and ears and hair' (five-year-old girl)

'On the bum, on the arm, on the leg [and on the] hand' (six-year-old boy)

'The ear or they just smack them across the leg... or pinch the leg' (five-year-old girl)

'On my bum, on my face, on my head and on my arm and on the belly and on the legs' (five-year-old girl)

'On the arm, and maybe on the hand' (six-year-old girl)

'They could be smacked on the leg or the bottom' (six-year-old girl)

'On your hand' Anywhere else? *'On your leg'* (six-year-old boy)

'And sometimes on your back' (six-year-old boy)

'On the back' Anywhere else? *'Round here [points to tummy]'* (six-year-old boy)

'On your tummy' (six-year-old)

'Sometimes on your bum, sometimes your leg and sometimes on your head' (seven-year-old girl)

'It's usually on your bottom or on your hands or beside your arm' (seven-year-old boy)

'They usually get smacked on the bottom or the hand or the side of their arms or on the side of them' (seven-year-old girl)

'I think they normally get smacked on the bottom or the arm' (seven-year-old boy)

'On their hands, on their back and their bum' (seven-year-old girl)

'On the bum, on their arm, on their back, on their leg, tummy [and] head' (seven-year-old girl)

Q5. What does it feel like to be smacked?

What it feels like to be smacked	Frequency (no. of different children who gave this answer)
It hurts, it's hard and makes you sore	58
It makes you feel miserable/sad/unhappy/upset/grumpy	26
I don't like it/it's horrible	17
It makes you cry	10
It stings/it itches/it gives you rashes	7
It makes you angry	2
You feel bruised/bitten	2
It makes you go red	2
It makes you feel bad/guilty	2
It's like someone's punched/kicked you	2
It makes you feel ashamed/embarrassed	2
You feel you're going to get grounded	2
You feel like you want to run away	2
It makes you feel nice	1
It's bumpy	1
It feels like someone's banged you with a hammer	1
It's like you're bleeding	1
It's like breaking your bones	1
It makes you not like your parents	1
It makes you feel sorry	1
It's soft	1
It feels uncomfortable	1

This question was answered in two ways. First, children described the physical sensations of being smacked and, second, they talked about how smacking makes them feel 'inside'.

The overwhelming message is that smacking hurts and that children do not like the feeling of being smacked – not just the physical pain but the emotional impact too. Within the confines of this question alone, 58 children told us that smacking hurts; this message also came through in other sections of the group discussions. Clearly adults do intend to hurt children when they smack; children's responses to this question suggest that those adults who set out to hurt are in fact usually successful in achieving this.

Many children vividly described the physical pain inflicted by smacking:

> *'It feels like someone banged you with a hammer.'* (five-year-old girl)

'[It feels] like someone's punched you or kicked you or something.' (six-year-old boy)
'It hurts and it's painful inside – it's like breaking your bones.' (seven-year-old girl)
'It's like when you're in the sky and you're falling to the ground and you just hurt yourself.'
(seven-year-old boy)

The emotional impact is described too:

'[Children feel] grumpy and sad and also really upset inside.' (five-year-old girl)
'It feels like you don't really like it, so it hurts and you cry.' Do you feel anything else inside?
'A sort of thing which pushes up and down and goes back.' (seven-year-old boy)
'[It] hurts your feelings inside.' (seven-year-old girl)

Children explained how smacking can negatively affect children's relationships with parents:

*'When you get smacked sometimes we get angry because sometimes when my mum smacks me you
get angry.'* (six-year-old boy)
'...and you feel you don't like your parents anymore.' (seven-year-old girl)
*'It feels, you feel sort of as though you want to run away because they're sort of like being mean
to you and it hurts a lot.'* (seven-year-old girl)

Asking for help does not always work: a five-year-old girl explained *'it feels bad or sad when
your dad or mum smacks you – you try and tell your aunties but they do nothing'*.

Some children also describe feeling embarrassed and ashamed:

*'It feels like [they] shouldn't have done that, it hurts. It feels embarrassed, it feels like you are really
sorry and it hurts.'* (seven-year-old girl)
'I think it probably makes you feel ashamed inside.' (seven-year-old girl)

The answers to this particular question were striking in that children we listened to vividly
portrayed both the emotional and physical impact of smacking:

'It hurts people and it doesn't feel nice and people don't like it when they are smacked.' (five-year-old)
'[It makes you] grumpy and sad and also really upset inside. And really hurt' (five-year-old girl)
'You're hurt and it makes you cry [and] drips come out of your eyes.' (five-year-old girl)

What does it feel like to be smacked: key themes and discussion points

Children talked about the physical and emotional impact of being smacked. The question
invited children to comment about both aspects of the experience. As can be seen from
children's responses, smacking physically hurts and has an emotional impact too. One of
the strongest messages from this question was that a smack is deeply felt by children.
Many of the children we listened to were clearly drawing on their own experiences.

What does it feel like to be smacked
A selection of quotes from children

It hurts, it's hard and it makes you sore

'What does it feel like to be smacked?'

'It hurts a lot, it makes you unhappy' (six-year-old girl)

'It hurts..if they smack you really hard, you cry' (seven-year-old girl)

'It feels hurt inside' (five-year-old girl)

'It hurts' (five-year-old boy)

'Hurting' Anything else? *'Sore, achy'* (five-year-old boy)

'It hurts' What does it feel like inside? *'bruised'* (five-year-old girl)

'Hard – bumpy' (five-year-old boy)

'Red [and] sore' (five-year-old boy)

'Don't know, it really hurts and sometimes they feel like they don't like smacks' (five-year-old boy)

'Well, it hurts. And when you get smacked you usually get smacked on the top part and that usually hurts most. So, I think it would probably hurt quite a lot but after two minutes or something it doesn't really hurt anymore' (six-year-old girl)

'Quite painful, [it] doesn't feel very nice and [it] can hurt you and make you feel sore' (six-year-old boy)

'Sometimes when I get smacked it feels like it hurts' (six-year-old boy)

'It's hard and it might be painful' (six-year-old boy)

'Not very nice' Why's that? *'Because it hurts you a lot and you might get a bruise or something'* And how does it feel inside? *'Horrible'* (six-year-old boy)

'It feels hard' How do you think children feel inside? *'Very very hurt'* (seven-year-old girl)

'Erm horrible and not very nice because it hurts you a lot' How does it feel inside? *'Sad'* (seven-year-old girl)

'It hurts you' It hurts you? *'It hurts your feelings inside'* (seven-year-old girl)

'It feels it hurts a lot and it hurts especially just there [points to upper thigh]' (seven-year-old boy)

'Painful [and] sad' (seven-year-old girl)

'It hurts and makes you feel sad' (seven-year-old girl)

'It feels very hard [and] sore' (seven-year-old girl)

It makes you feel miserable, sad, unhappy, upset and grumpy

'Sad and they cry and they cry and they cry and cry' (five-year-old girl)

'It feels like something what you really don't like. It makes you cry' (six-year-old boy)

'Sad' (five-year-old boy & girl)

Unkind' Unkind? *'Uhh, all sad. You cry and you're miserable'* (five-year-old boy)

'It feels upsetting and it really feels uncomfortable. It feels sore' (five-year-old girl)

'You feel sad' (six-year-old girl)

'Not very nice' (six-year-old boy)

'It feels painful'

'It makes you cry' (seven-year-old boy)

'It doesn't feel very nice inside. And you might be upset' (seven-year-old girl)

'It's horrible' What do you think children feel like? *'Sad'* (seven-year-old girl)

It stings, itches and gives you rashes

'It feels a bit stingy and [it] itches a bit' (seven-year-old boy)
'It kind of feels horrid, it just feels horrid, you know, and it really hurts, it stings you and makes you horrible inside... I think it probably makes you feel ashamed inside' (seven-year-old girl)
'Sometimes it stings. It hurts. And sometimes they might tell on you when you didn't do nothing, and you get a smack' (seven-year-old boy)

'Yeh and erm it hurts your feelings and inside it gives you rashes and stuff on you' (seven-year-old boy)

You feel bruised or bitten

'Well. It hurts a lot. And it feels like you're bitten by something' What does it feel like inside? *'It hurts your feelings'* (six-year-old girl)

It makes you feel bad

'You feel bad and guilty'
'Because you've done something wrong' (six-year-old boy)

You feel like you want to run away

'Sad and like running away' (seven-year-old girl)

Children feel nice

'Inside [it's] nice to be smacked, [it] just stings and [it's] quite nice' (six-year-old boy)

It's soft

'Its hard and sometimes it can be soft' (six-year-old girl)

Q6a. How do children act after they have been smacked?

Children's response to being smacked	Frequency (no. of different children who gave this answer)
Cry/scream/be upset/feel sad or hurt	32
Go to bed/their bedroom/be alone for a while/avoid adults	30
Be naughty/cheeky/nasty	14
Try to do something right/be good/make amends	13
Get angry/grumpy/cross	10
Say sorry	5
Scared they might get hit again/they get hit again	4
Feel tired/go to sleep	2
Feel they're bad/naughty	2
Smack back	2
Smack somebody else (not the person who smacked them)	2
Tell someone	2
Feel really embarrassed	2
Play	2
Learn from their mistake	1
Do the same mistake again	1
Get sent to stand on the stairs	1
Think parents are silly	1
Feel relieved afterwards	1
Feel ashamed	1
Think it's OK to smack	1
They think it's funny that they've been smacked	1
Refuse to eat food	1

There were two aspects to children's responses to this question: first they described what children *do* after they have been smacked; second, they explained how children *feel* after they have been smacked.

Children's views on what children do after being smacked included: crying and being upset; being naughty, cheeky or nasty; trying to make amends; going, or being sent, to their bed/bedroom; spending time alone; smacking back; smacking somebody else; being quiet; telling someone; getting another smack; doing the same mistake again; being sent to stand on the stairs; going to sleep; and saying sorry.

Children described a range of feelings which are aroused after children are smacked. These included: being upset and feeling sad; feeling angry, grumpy and cross; fear that they might get hit again; feel they are bad or naughty; feel really embarrassed; think parents are silly; feel relieved afterwards; and being ashamed. A five-year-old suggested that children might think it's funny they have been smacked while another said children might pretend to cry. These untypical responses imply that even very young children may sometimes try to underrate the impact of being hit – a factor more commonly associated with grown adults.

How do children act after they have been smacked: key themes and discussion points

The top three responses to this question were: children cry and become upset; children go or are sent to their bedroom or spend time alone; and children act naughty or cheeky after they have been smacked. This suggests that, from children's perspectives, smacking hurts their feelings, has a negative effect on behaviour and harms their relationships with those who smack them. It also shows that children associate smacking with being at home.

How do children act after they have been smacked? A selection of quotes from children

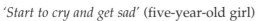

'How do children act after being smacked?'

They are upset, sad and hurt

'They cry, also they weep [and] they might think their parents are silly' (five-year-old girl)

'Cry, and sometimes if they haven't got a handle on their door in their bedrooms – like I haven't – they lock themselves inside' (five-year-old boy)

'Start to cry and get sad' (five-year-old girl)
'Children stand up and cry' (five-year-old boy)
'Sometimes may feel that inside like their tummy hurts' (five-year-old boy)
'Sometimes they be cheeky, they cry, they tell the people outside, they tell everyone else even their mums parents and all the family – the lot – and your mum gives you another smack and you tell your family again and again and you keep on getting hit again and again' (six-year-old boy)
'They scream and cry on the bed' (six-year-old boy)
'They cry and they moan at their mums. They say 'why did you smack me mum?' in a moany voice' (six-year-old girl)
'They might go up to their room and cry' (seven-year-old girl)
'They feel sad and they play with the people they're allowed to play with and they don't do the naughty thing again and they don't fight with people and they don't do naughty things' (seven-year-old boy)
'Erm, they usually start crying and they sort of try not to go near the adults again but they have to. They don't really like speaking for another two minutes. If they are at home they get sent to the stairs for five minutes' Why do you think the children cry then after they have been smacked? 'Because it hurts, and they feel ashamed' (seven-year-old girl)

They go or are sent to their bedroom; they spend time alone

'Sometimes they run up to their bedrooms and just read a book on their bed when they've calmed down a bit' (seven-year-old girl)

'Run to their bedroom and sulk on their beds' (five-year-old girl)

'Go to sleep' (five-year-old boy)

'They go to their rooms and they cry' (six-year-old girl)

'Go up to their bedrooms' (seven-year-old boy)

'Sometimes they get sent to bed. They start crying. And sometimes I get sent to bed and I get no tea later' (six-year-old boy)

'They go and have a bath, they get their pyjamas on and then go to bed' (five-year-old girl)

'They might go up to their bedrooms and cry and be on their own' So they'll be on their own? *'Because they might smack them back'* Who might smack them back? *'The person who's been sent to bed because he's been so angry because he's got smacked hard'* (six-year-old boy)

'They might cry, they might get upset and they might have to go to bed' (six-year-old girl)

'They cry and their mum sends them up to put their pyjamas on and go to bed' (six-year-old girl)

'Well, if they get smacked and sent upstairs and then play on the computer and your parents hear it they might come up, open your door and they might smack you' So what would you do after being smacked? *'Cry'* (six-year-old boy)

'They cry and their mums might tell them to go to bed and get their pyjamas on' (seven-year-old girl)

'Start crying and get sent to bed' (seven-year-old girl)

'And if your mum or dad say go to your room you might not go' (seven-year-old boy)

They do something naughty, cheeky or nasty

'Some of them if they're really naughty they do the same mistake again and if they're good they learn from their mistake' (six-year-old boy)

'they act naughty and start to hurt people...they're very angry and the adult thinks they can do as he wants' (five-year-old girl)

'once they've been smacked they start being nasty to their mum or dad again...some children think they gets their own way' (five-year-old girl)

'they act cheeky to their mums...they think it's funny they've been smacked' (five-year-old girl)

'they be naughty again...they're very naughty' (four-year-old boy)

'And when you're having a drink you might spill it on purpose' (six-year-old boy)

'Uh, throw things on the floor – because they're really naughty' (seven-year-old girl)

'Erm go up to their rooms and they might do something like they might break something or hurt their parents' Why might they hurt their parents? *'It's like getting your own back. It's a bit silly cos they might do it again'* (seven-year-old girl)

'Kick chairs, rip things [and] push their mummy's over' (seven-year-old girl)

'Pull faces when your mum and dad are not looking' (seven-year-old boy)

'Some run up to their bedrooms and throw a tantrum [they] scream' (seven-year-old girl)

'Running round the room and stuff' Why do they do that? *'because they've hurt theirself badly'* How have they hurt themselves? *'By being naughty and their mums smacking them around here [points to thigh] and it hurts them so much they just run around knocking chairs down and stuff and pushing all the furniture down'* (seven-year-old boy)

They try to make amends

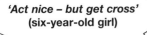

'Good because they don't want to be smacked again' (six-year-old girl)

'Be good' (five-year-old boy)

'When my mum shouts at me and then I cried when I was in the passage at my nanny's house and when they've been smacked they pretend to cry. And they weep and then they go in a room and tidy up what their mother said and then they read a book' (five-year-old girl)

'Could be really good because [they] know they've been naughty' (six-year-old boy)

'Very good because [they] want to get a reward' (six-year-old girl)

'Try and do their hardest to try and get it right or don't do it again' (seven-year-old girl)

'Sometimes they just keep quiet, because they feel really embarrassed and sometimes they just try to be good and try to do the best thing...it actually depends what you have been smacked for. If they have been very naughty just making, let's say, making a mess all over the kitchen, then they probably just try and go tidy it up and keep quiet about it. If they whacked someone in the face or something then they just kind of say sorry and make up and go and play with them or just keep quiet and be on their own' (seven-year-old girl)

'I don't know, but...they might cry a bit or try and make up for it and try to behave' (seven-year-old girl)

'Act nice – but get cross' (six-year-old girl)

'Be much much nicer because [otherwise] they will get smacked over and over again' (seven-year-old girl)

'they're going to be good to their mams and dads' (seven-year-old girl)

They get angry, grumpy and cross

'mad, slam the door' (six-year-old boy)

'They get angry and grumpy and cross with their mummies' (five-year-old girl)

'They start to feel bad-tempered and they start to wander around the room' Do they do anything else? *'They might go up to their bedroom and throw themselves onto the bed'* Why would they throw themselves onto the bed? *'Because they're bad-tempered'* (six-year-old girl)

'They might stamp so hard and if you've got a board floor, they might break it. They might say sorry and do it again' (seven-year-old girl)

'Cry or go up to their room and throw things about' Why might they throw things about? *'Because they feel angry'* (seven-year-old girl)

'Well, they go up to their room and be bad-tempered. And then they go all hot or something like that' Why do you think they go all hot? *'Because they're angry'* (seven-year-old boy)

They say sorry/regret what they have done

'Cry, chuck stones or just say sorry. If they bumped into somebody they say just say sorry' (five-year-old boy)

'They cry and they feel they're naughty and they wish they'd never done it...and they start to be good' And what's being good? *'Doing as you're told, tidying your bedroom and cleaning up'* (seven-year-old boy)

'They say sorry and don't do it again for a long time' (seven-year-old girl)

They get smacked again, or fear being smacked again

'They have a bath, they don't ask their mum or their daddy. They have a bath, they put the clothes on, they put their shoes on and go outside and dad finds them and smacks them. [Afterwards] the children say sorry' (five-year-old girl)

'I think they act a bit shy and don't go near bigger people than themselves, because they stand there and after a few minutes go down and play again' Why do the children not go near the bigger people? *'Because they are scared'* What are they scared of? *'Because they might get smacked again'* (seven-year-old boy)

They feel they are bad

'Feel they're bad' (seven-year-old boy)

They smack back

'When they have been smacked then sometimes [they] smack their mum' (five-year-old boy)

'I think sometimes they might smack their parents back because they did it to them so they think it's a good idea to do it back. And they might go to their bedroom and be on their own for a while and do something in the bedroom for a while and stop being cross and then their parents will stop being cross to them' (six-year-old girl)

They smack somebody else

'Smack somebody else' (five-year-old boy)

'I've thought of another answer – if they're very little, they might think it's right to smack and go off and smack somebody else' (seven-year-old girl)

They refuse to eat food

'They won't eat their dinner' (seven-year-old boy)

Q6b. How do adults act after they have given a smack?

What adults do after they have given a smack	Frequency no. of different children who gave this answer
Get cross/grumpy/look mad/faces go red	27
Feel sorry/regret what they've done/feel guilty/sad/upset/bad	22
Carry on with what they were doing before	9
Smack child again/act as if they want to hit again	6
Ignore child	5
Take away pocket money/toys/drinks/sweets/special outings	5
Take or send the child to bed/bedroom	5
Feel pleased/good/happy/laugh	5
Make child miss a meal/delay a meal	4
Shout/swear/tell the child off	4
Feel ashamed of the child/upset at child	3
Lock child in bedroom	2
Stop child going outside/ground them	1
Pull faces/make gesture at the child	1
Grab the child	1
Have some peace	1
Give the child a hiding	1
Hit child on head	1
Give child another chance	1

Children associated being smacked with angry or bad-tempered adults: many of them said that adults get cross or 'look mad' after they have given a smack. A seven-year-old girl said adults' faces turn 'beetroot' when they are mad; a five-year-old said *'they sort of walk around very fast'*; and a four-year-old boy said adults who smack *'get a grumpy face, like that [shows teeth]'*. Others mentioned adults shouting or swearing at them: a seven-year-old boy said adults might *'pull faces'* after they have smacked, or *'put their middle finger up at you'*.

The children we listened to had detailed insights into how adults might feel after they have smacked children. Interestingly, a large number of children said that adults feel sorry, or regret their actions. A seven-year-old girl said, *'I think they feel a bit sort of sorry but they don't want to say, but they do'*. Another seven-year-old girl explained that adults often believe they are doing the right thing when they smack, *'they wished they hadn't done it but they know it's because they just had to do it and they probably feel ashamed at their child.'* A five-year-old girl suggested, *'they don't feel like they wanted to smack in the first place'*.

A few gave examples of parents apologising to children and taking them to the park, the beach or buying them sweets. Five children said they thought adults felt pleased with themselves or happy after they have smacked children; a five-year-old said adults sometimes laugh afterwards. This may signify that children believe adults view smacking as a positive and justified activity, or it may be an example of children recalling how their parents look or behave after they have smacked.

Nine children described adults immediately returning to what they were doing after they have smacked children – examples include queueing for a Lottery ticket, talking to their friends at the front doorstep, watching television, eating a meal and shopping. A six-year-old boy explained, *'if they're outside the door talking to someone then they could just come in and smack you and then go out again'*.

Two children explained that if children's bedroom doors have keyholes then their parents might lock them in. One child said adults might grab the child, another said they might give them a hiding and a seven-year-old boy said adults act stupid and *'hit you on the head where they're not supposed to hit you'*. Some children said that adults hit again after they have smacked a first time. The reasons children usually gave for this were that they had disobeyed their parents, for example playing with toys or computer games when they had been sent to their bedroom as a punishment, *'when you're throwing stones they might give you a smack. And you might have to go inside and go to your bedroom and you might not be allowed to play on your computer or your megadrive. And if you do, then you get another one'* (seven-year-old girl).

Five children talked about adults ignoring them after they have smacked them. A six-year-old girl explained, *'well, they usually are still quite cross and if you need them afterwards they don't really reply. They just keep on doing what they do'*.

**How do adults act after they have given a smack:
key themes and discussion points**

The children we listened to seemed to associate smacking with angry parents and many said they thought parents regretted hitting afterwards.

This question encouraged children to empathise with adults and think about their actions and feelings. While equally valuable, some responses are drawn from their own direct experiences, whereas others are more likely to be based on children's observations.

How do adults act after they have given a smack?
A selection of quotes from children

They feel or act angry

'Sometimes they are angry and slam things down' (seven-year-old girl)

'They sort of walk around very fast and being cross' (seven-year-old girl)

'They get angry. They are cross' (five-year-old girl)

'They feel angry, [they have an] angry face, like a sad face' (five-year-old girl)

'Cross with the children' (five-year-old boy)

'Shout' (five-year-old boy)

'You know they feel a bit cross and they tell you to go upstairs. They [the children] might stamp their feet and they come up and smack you again' (six-year-old boy)

'Well, they usually are still quite cross and if you need them afterwards they don't really reply. They just keep on doing what they do' (six-year-old girl)

'They shout and they scream and they cry' (six-year-old girl)

'And the grown ups get cross' (seven-year-old boy)

'I think they feel that they feel quite cross that the child has done it and they are sad that they have had to do it but sometimes some adults don't really think it is better that they done it than just let the child go being naughty' (seven-year-old girl)

'Well, they act cross and they say something like don't you ever do that again and they might smack you again' Why do you think they'd smack again? 'Because they've got even angrier' (seven-year-old boy)

'They look a bit cross because of what they've done' (seven-year-old girl)

They regret smacking or say sorry

'They send you to watch TV. They feel like they'll never do it again' (six-year-old girl)

'And they sometimes feel they want to say sorry' (five-year-old boy)

'Guilty' (five-year-old girl)

'Want to say sorry' (five-year-old girl)

'They kind of they say sorry to their children then the children say sorry to the parents and then if they be good they go to the pub with their parents' (five-year-old girl)

'They say sorry to the children and they went to the beach' (five-year-old girl)

'They feel sorry' (five-year-old girl)

'They feel sorry and...they went to the shop and buy them a teddy bear' (five-year-old girl)

'They say sorry to their children and also the children say sorry to the grown ups' (five-year-old girl)

'They feel sorry and they go where the kids are and they go up the stairs and open the door and they say sorry to the kids and the children say 'that's alright' and they go to the park' (five-year-old girl)

'They feel sorry and they went to the shop and the mum said to the dad "buy a present" and she says sorry to the adults' (five-year-old girl)

> **'They feel sorry for the children and they go up and say sorry'**
> (five-year-old girl)

'We might do something yeh then their friend might tell our mum then our mum gives us a smack and don't let us play out any more then she feels that she shouldn't give us a smack cos that was just a little thing' (six-year-old boy)

'Sometimes they feel that they should give you another one' Why do they feel they should give you another one? *'Because they feel reluctant to give you another one'* Do you know why they feel reluctant? *'Because you are their child they don't really want to smack you and say if they smack a child the child will keep on telling people and people will tell people and other people will tell the police and it goes round and round the world and then the police might come and arrest your mum or your dad'* (six-year-old boy)

'I think...they also feel they shouldn't have done, but they know that they should have done it because the child was naughty but they feel ashamed they did it and ashamed with their child' (seven-year-old boy)

'They might feel sorry for themselves and get you a present and take you to your favourite restaurant' Why might they give you another smack? *'Because you've done the same thing again and you said sorry already'* And why might they take you out and feel sorry? *'Because they might not have wanted to do it but they felt like doing it'* (seven-year-old girl)

> **'They finish eating their breakfast or their supper'**
> (seven-year-old girl)

'Erm they might send you up to your room. Or they might, if you've done something by accident that you didn't mean to, they might say sorry' (seven-year-old girl)

They continue what they were doing before they smacked

'Go downstairs and get on [with] what they were doing' (five-year-old boy)

'Carry on doing what they were doing. They're a bit upset that their child's done it' (seven-year-old girl)

'They feel bad and they carry on doing what they were doing before' (seven-year-old)

They might shout, swear or smack again

> **'They might give you another one'**
> (seven-year-old girl)

'I think when your mum or your dad give you a smack, you might go upstairs and stamp your feet and your mum might shout at you, and if you keep on doing it she might give you another smack' (six-year-old girl)

'Sometimes they swear, sometimes they swear' (six-year-old boy)

They ignore children

'Well, they tell them off again and they won't talk to them. They'll just get on with their work that they were doing' (six-year-old girl)

'They sometimes, my mum she doesn't really talk to us much if we ask anything, she feels cross and she's not very pleased' (seven-year-old girl)

'They feel they don't want to talk to you, they feel they are getting back to a sulky mood' (seven-year-old girl)

They stop children playing with their friends or take away treats

'If you ask them something they may not answer and they might not let you go outside, or have something you really want like something for dinner' Why do you think that adults might go quiet? *'Because you've been naughty'* (seven-year-old girl)

'Won't let you have any sweets' (seven-year-old girl)

'If they've given you a smack like because you've broken something – if you were going to go out to a party or something, they won't let you go' (seven-year-old girl)

> *'They're quiet and they'll not let you play outside with your friends [and] they won't let your friends come to the house'* (seven-year-old girl)

They take toys or other possessions away

'When children have got pocket money they sometimes take their pocket money away' (five-year-old girl)

> *'They will take some toys away and only have a little bit of toys. They might take all your money, jewellery and everything except your bed'* (five-year-old girl)

They send children to their rooms

'Your mum sends you upstairs until your dinner and you're only allowed to come back downstairs when it's dinner time. And then after your dinner you go back up' (six-year-old girl)

They are pleased or happy

'Adults are quite pleased because they've told the children off' (six-year-old)

'Good because they've done what they should have done' (six-year-old)

> *'Happy because children won't do it again'* (six-year-old)

Q7a. Why don't children smack adults?

Reason why children don't smack adults	**Frequency** no. of different children who gave this answer
Too frightened/don't want to get smacked back	29
Don't want to get told off/sent upstairs/punished	20
Adults don't deserve to be smacked; they're more grown up/only adults have permission to smack/children are too little/too young to smack	13
Adults are bigger/adults can hit harder	10
It's naughty/rude/bad manners/out of order	10
Grown ups are older	8
Children do smack adults sometimes	4
It won't help/children don't want to	4
It might cause a fight	2
No-one should smack anyone	1
Children know what it feels like	1
Adults don't like being smacked	1

The most frequent answer to why children don't smack adults is that children are too scared: a large proportion of children said children fear being hit back. As one six-year-old girl explained, *'because if they smack adults the adults smack them back and it hurts'*.

Many children said that adults are bigger and so can hit harder than them: a seven-year-old girl said *'adults are bigger and the adults can smack harder than children'*. A six-year-old boy said that children may want to smack adults *'because they feel cross and mad, but they [don't because they] think the adult is going to smack you back really hard'*. One seven-year-old boy was eager to answer this question: *'That's simple! Because it's very rude to smack your parents because they're bigger and older and they might hurt you back and they might be silly when they're drunk and they might hit you'*.

Later in our discussions a seven-year-old boy, talking about why it is wrong to smack, revealed what it can feel like to be hit by a much bigger person, *'and sometimes if you smack, if it was an adult like my daddy, he can smack very hard...he can smack you like a stone...and you'll cry'*.

Twenty children said that they thought children don't smack adults because they might be punished in a non-physical way such as being told off, sent to their bedroom or grounded. Some children mentioned that children are too little or too young to smack. A five-year-old girl explained that children might feel like smacking adults but they cannot; *'because the children lost their temper and they think they're adults but they're not, they're just children'*. A seven-year-old girl alluded to children's relatively low status, *'adults are bigger and stronger and people treat them more seriously'*. Another seven-year-old explained that children don't smack adults, *'because adults are older than children and you deserve a smack if you get on adults' nerves'*.

Other children specifically stated that children do not smack adults because it is wrong. Another two children said it might hurt the grown up and a five-year-old girl said that no-one should smack anyone. A seven-year-old girl said she doesn't smack adults because *'I'll get the hang of it and it won't help really'.*

Four children said children do smack adults – a five-year-old boy described hitting his dad in the bathroom because he was hitting his mum. Another six-year-old said, *'I do smack my mum and then they don't smack me back. Because I only play'.*

Why don't children smack adults: key themes and discussion points

The children we listened to said children do not smack adults for two main reasons: they don't want to be smacked back; and they don't want to be punished in a non-physical way. Differences between the size, and physical strength, of adults and children was commonly referred to in this question.

It could be argued that children not hitting because they themselves do not wish to be hit is a sign that smacking works as a deterrent, and has a positive effect on shaping children's behaviour. Conversely, the message could be that a primary factor influencing whether children retaliate when hit is whether the person who hits them is bigger and stronger, rather than a general rejection and capacity to resolve conflict without violence.

Children's comments about smacking adults being 'bad manners' or 'out of order' may demonstrate that a significant number of children believe smacking is wrong and/or that they may respect adults more than adults respect them (see question 9b).

**Why don't children smack adults?
A selection of quotes from children**

Because they might get smacked back

Adults smack children but why don't children smack adults?

'Cos adults can probably hit children harder' (seven-year-old boy)

'Because if the children smack the adults the adults will smack them back even harder' (five-year-old girl)

'Because adults would slap them back and they would get really angry' (six-year-old girl)

'They might get smacked again' (five-year-old girl)
'Because they smack back' (five-year-old boy)
'Because they will smack them back' (five-year-old boy)
'I don't think they'd do it back because then they might get smacked again' (six-year-old girl)
'If the children smacks the adult, the adult will get cross and the adult...will smack the children and the children will start crying' (six-year-old girl)

'I sometimes smack my mum or my dad when I am really cross but the reason they probably don't smack adults is they are afraid they might get really hurt or they might get sent up [stairs] or maybe it is just that they don't want to do it' (seven-year-old)

'If you smack the adult, the adult will smack you back and then you'll start crying and they won't' Why won't they start crying? *'Because they're brave'* (seven-year-old girl)

'Because they are too frightened to smack their parents because they've just given them a smack and they don't want to get smacked' (seven-year-old)

'Because they might smack them back' (seven-year-old girl)

'Because they might smack the adult really hard and the adult might fall over and break something, then the adult would smack her again' (seven-year-old girl)

'Well, if the adults are really cross and the child tries to smack them, it might just smack it back. Then you might be sent up to your bedroom' (seven-year-old boy)

'Because they'll get another smack' (seven-year-old girl)

'Because the adults will just hit them back' (seven-year-old boy)

'Because adults might hit them even harder' (seven-year-old boy)

Because they might get told off or punished

'Might get told off really badly, or locked in [a] room, [or] a favourite toy might get taken away' (six-year-old)

'They might be frightened that the adults are going to tell them off for doing that or they might get an even bigger punishment' (seven-year-old)

'Because if they smack the adult back they'll get into trouble' (five-year-old boy)

'Because they might get told off' (six-year-old)

'Because they might get told off, because mummy will get cross with them' (six-year-old)

'Because...if they did that they might get punished or grounded' (six-year-old boy)

'Because they smacked back and they send them back into their bedroom again. And if they have a keyhole on their door the adults might lock them in' (six-year-old boy)

'They might smack the adult and the adult might send them to bed' (six-year-old girl)

'Because they'd get told off again. If they'd do it again, they'd get two, they'd do it back' (seven-year-old girl)

'They are probably not going to do it to adults because they are scared of the adults doing something and telling them off' (seven-year-old)

'Because they'll just smack them back and they'll get told off and stuff' (seven-year-old girl)

'They might get sent to bed or get grounded' (seven-year-old boy)

Because adults are older, bigger or more grown up

'Because they're too big' Who are too big? *'Grown ups'* Any other reasons why children don't smack adults? *'Because they can shout at yer'* (six-year-old boy)

'Because the adults are the children's father' (six-year-old boy)

'Because grown ups are older than us' (six-year-old boy)

'I think it is because they are also bigger than children' (seven-year-old)

'Because the fathers and mothers are bigger than the children' (six-year-old boy)

'Because adults are more grown up' (five-year-old girl)

Because it's naughty, rude or bad manners

'Because they didn't like what grown ups did to them' (six-year-old girl)

'Because they get a grumpy face – their daddy's and their nannies' (four-year-old boy)
'Because adults might get a bit cross' (five-year-old boy)
'They might get a bit angry' (five-year-old girl)
'Because that's out of order' (five-year-old girl)
'Children don't smack adults because otherwise they would get told off and you shouldn't smack your mum or your dad – no one should smack anyone' (five-year-old girl)
'Because it makes them feel not nice inside' (five-year-old girl)
'Because it's naughty' (five-year-old boy)
'Because it's naughty. And when their dad smacks them back they don't ever do it again' (six-year-old girl)
'Because it's not right and they are not supposed to' (six-year-old girl)
'Because it's naughty' (seven-year-old girl)

Because adults and children are treated and behave differently

'Because little children aren't bigger than adults but the adults are bigger than them, so the adults can smack the little ones and the little ones can't smack the adults' (five-year-old girl)
'Because they are too little' (seven-year-old boy)
'Because they're too young to smack older people – you shouldn't smack older people than you' (seven-year-old boy)
'Because they shouldn't be allowed to – they're too young' (seven-year-old boy)

They do!

'Because if they're older than you they've got the permission to smack' (seven-year-old boy)

'Because when the adults or the dad be rude to the children the dad runs away [and] the girl smacks his bum' (five-year-old girl)
'Cos sometimes they do if they are not very nice' (seven-year-old boy)

Because it won't help

'When you smack the adult, they might smack you again, and you might smack them back and they might smack you back and you'll smack them back. Then you'll keep going like that til bedtime like you're still going like that' (six-year-old boy)
'They might not have done it but when it's all over thought, actually, I wanted to' So, children might think about smacking adults? *'[I] might think wow, they shouldn't be smacking me [and] I start smacking them and I'll get the hang of it and it won't help really'* (seven-year-old girl)
'I think when a little girl or a little boy gets told off the dad or the mum will smack them and they might smack them back and then they have to go upstairs, go to bed and then they might have to go to sleep. And instead of going to sleep you might mess about in bed and your grown up might smack you again and you carry on smacking again' (seven-year-old girl)

Because adults don't like it

'Because they don't like it' Who doesn't like it? *'The adult'* (five-year-old boy)

Q7b. Why don't adults smack each other?

Reasons why adults don't smack each other	Frequency no. of different children who gave this answer
Adults are older – they know better	12
They're not kids/they're too big/only children get smacked	11
They're friends/married/love each other/they respect each other	11
Adults don't want to smack each other/they might hurt each other	11
It's rude/naughty/silly/bad manners/it's not very nice	7
Adults are not naughty	4
Adults don't want to start a fight	3
Adults do smack each other sometimes	3
Adults don't get cross with each other/tell each other off	3
Children will copy	3
It's embarrassing	3
The other adult might leave	2
Adults only get cross with each other	2
Adults argue instead	2
Adults are not allowed to smack each other/the police will come	2
Adults don't get as angry as children do	1
Adults aren't nasty to each other	1

Most children answered this question by comparing adults and children, which is not surprising given the way we structured the question. The most frequent reason children gave for adults not smacking each other was that adults are bigger and know better. Some children referred to adults being able to control themselves better than children; a seven-year-old girl explained, *'we don't know really that well and we just get so cross that we just do it without thinking and these adults they know better and they know it would be rude...and as children we don't do it wherever we are, it just seems to be a reaction'*. She further explains why adults don't smack each other:

> *'Grown ups don't smack each other because...they are older and they know better and let's say there were two people, one got very cross with someone, they smack them and then it would be very naughty and they would feel very embarrassed and the reason children smack each other is because they are in a kind of habit. Grown ups grow out of the habit and if they still have the habit they don't smack each other, instead they smack children.'*

Eleven children said that adults don't smack each other because they love each other, are friends or respect each other. A five-year-old girl said, *'because they must respect each other cos if they smacked each other they won't like each other'*; another explained, *'because they're friends*

and they like to be friends with each other and not smack each other and not argue with each other'.
A six-year-old boy said adults don't smack each other because they *'are really good friends'*
and a five-year-old boy suggested that the reason is *'because they go to bed with each other and
they need each other and they sleep together. They give a cuddle and they give a kiss and they shout
at each other'.*

Some children said that adults do not want to hurt each other, or start a fight while three said
it would be embarrassing. Adults actively choosing *not* to hit each other was mentioned
often. Interestingly only a few children suggested that adults do not smack each other
because they are not naughty. We can therefore conclude that, from children's perspective,
adults do not smack each other because they have made a conscious decision not to.

A few children challenged the question itself and said that adults do smack each other,
recalling instances where their parents were fighting. A five-year-old boy explained, *'my
mum and dad have smacked each other because daddy was doing hard things to mum. And I kicked
him, and I smacked him and kicked him'.*

Why don't adults smack each other: key themes and discussion points

This question uncovered a lot about children's insights into adult's behaviour and
relationships with each other. The three main responses to this question were: adults
know better; adults are too big to smack; and adults have special relationships which
would be negatively affected by smacking.

Some may doubt whether this question was fair as adults clearly do hit adults. There
were two main reasons why we phrased this question as we did. First, although there is
a great deal of inter-personal violence between adults, this is rarely – if ever – referred to
as smacking. We were interested to hear children's views on this. We also wanted to
encourage them to think about how adults deal with anger and frustration between
themselves, and to find out from children why they think adults do not routinely hit or
condone violence among 'grown ups'.

Why don't adults smack each other?
A selection of quotes from children

Because they know better

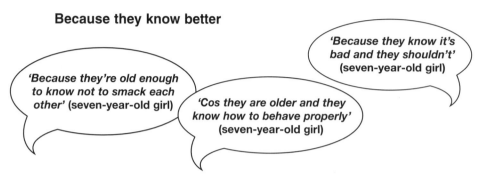

'Because they're old enough to know not to smack each other' (seven-year-old girl)

'Cos they are older and they know how to behave properly' (seven-year-old girl)

'Because they know it's bad and they shouldn't' (seven-year-old girl)

'Because it is rude, they are older, they know better, it will be embarrassing someone else and not your family. They can be cross with the other person but it is not very good to hit them'. (seven-year-old girl)
'Because they think the other person would smack the other adult and because they both know better so they don't smack each other' (seven-year-old boy)
'Because they're older and they think it is silly to smack each other' (seven-year-old girl)
'Children are naughty and think it's good to smack each other but adults are big and they know not to smack each other' (seven-year-old girl)
'Because probably they don't get as mad at each other because children have to learn and the adults should've learned that they shouldn't be fighting all the time so that's why they don't hardly um fight' (seven-year-old boy)
'Because the children erm they're young and they need to learn their lesson but the adults should have learnt it now so that's why they don't fall out as much and shout at each other as much. They should have learned their lesson' (seven-year-old boy)

Because they are not children and they are too old

'Because adults aren't nasty to each other' (five-year-old boy)

'Adults are too old to smack' (six-year-old)
'Adults are too grown up' (six-year-old)
'Because adults don't need to smack another adult because they're not like children' (six-year-old)

Because they respect and love each other, and they are friends

'Because they're friends. And because they love each other' (six-year-old girl)
'Because they both got married and they don't like smacking each other. They only get cross with each other' (six-year-old boy)
'Because they're both big and if they've got married, they don't' (six-year-old boy)
'I don't really know, but I think it might be because they are cross with each other but they are friends and they don't really want to so they just do other things but they don't smack' (six-year-old girl)
'Because they're both big and they only get cross with each other, they don't smack' (six-year-old girl)
'Adults don't smack each other because they're married and they don't smack each other because grown ups only sometimes get told off' (seven-year-old girl)

Because they don't want to smack each other

'Because they don't want to – it could hurt' (seven-year-old boy)

'Because they don't want to' (five-year-old boy)
'Because they might hurt each other' (five-year-old girl)
'Adults don't smack each [because] they don't like smacking each other' (five-year-old girl)
'Because it makes them feel not very nice' (five-year-old girl)
'Because...only children get smacked and grown ups don't want to get smacked' Why don't they want to get smacked? 'Because it hurts' (six-year-old)
'Because they don't want to and they're too big to smack each other' Oh, they're too big to smack each other? 'They only smack the children' (six-year-old girl)
'Well, instead of smacking each other, they argue and so in the end they decide to do the thing' (seven-year-old boy)

Because it's wrong to smack

'Because they're not allowed to' Why aren't they allowed to? 'Because it's bad manners' (five-year-old girl)
'Because it's naughty' (six-year-old boy)
'Because it's not very nice' (six-year-old girl)

Because adults are not naughty

'Because children are always naughty and adults are not' (six-year-old boy)
'Cos they're big and they don't want to smack each other...cos children are very naughty and they're not' (six-year-old girl)
'Because adults aren't usually naughty and grown ups don't start a fight' (seven-year-old girl)
'The adults aren't naughty and the children are, so the adults give the children a smack' (seven-year-old girl)

Because they want to avoid causing a fight

'Because if they smack each other then the other one will smack again...and they will get into a big fight and then when the next adult comes when the front door bell [rings] they come in the door [and] they'll act as if they've not beaten up and they don't want...them to recognise if they've been having a fight' (five-year-old girl)
'Because the other one would hit them and it would turn into a fight' (six-year-old boy)

Adults do smack each other

'They do because once my dad smacked my mum on her face' (six-year-old girl)

'Because they might smack each other, because they might be jealous of each other and they might not want to work with each other and they might get drunk and they might be smacking each other and my dad and my dad's friend – he's called Matt...[they] got drunk and they were smacking each other...I don't want people in the street seeing my dad fight with [his] friend' (six-year-old boy)

Because they don't get cross or tell each other off

'Because they might not get cross with each other' (six-year-old girl)

'Children smack each other because sometimes they might get cross with each other and they might smack each other' That's what children do, but what about adults? Why don't adults smack each other? *'Because grown ups don't get told off, because they don't tell each other off'* (seven-year-old girl)

'Because children will copy even more' (seven-year-old boy)

Because children will copy

'Because then the children will start to do it' (five-year-old boy)
'Cos the children will start doing it' (five-year-old boy)

Because the police would get involved

'Because the police would come' (five-year-old boy)

Q8. When you are big, will you smack children?

From the 72 children who answered this question:	no. of different children who gave this answer
Will not smack children when they are adults	36
Will smack children if they are naughty	27
Will depend on law	3
Not often/not a lot/sometimes	3
Don't know/unsure	2
Parents *have* to smack children	1

When we consider the different age groups, we can see that the younger children appeared to be less favourable towards smacking than their older counterparts. This may be related to children's experience of being hit (research shows that physical punishment is more prevalent among younger children – see pp 14-15), or it could be that older children have started to rationalise and take on commonly held adult attitudes that smacking is an inevitable part of parenting.

Age group	no. who answered question	no. of different children who say they will not smack when they are big
four and five-year-olds	21	13
six-year-olds	24	12
seven-year-olds	27	11

This question spurred children into listing a whole catalogue of misdemeanours which they say they will deal with by smacking when they are adults:

> **Examples of behaviour/actions which children believe they will smack for when they are adults**
>
> *Will smack children if they:* smack other people; pull hair; deliberately break things; take paper from a bin; beat somebody up; knock things over; won't stop crying; cry for nothing; steal; get new clothes muddy; throw stones; pinch/nip; kick; have chewing gum when they are not allowed; rip somebody's shirt; spit chewing gum on the carpet; go to places they are not allowed; throw a ball into neighbour's garden; accidentally squirt water onto an adult from a water pistol; swear; write or paint on walls; spill things; are in a bad mood because the adult has won at cricket.

In one group two boys, a six and seven-year-old, started a dialogue about smacking children. The seven-year-old, who had previously described in detail what it feels like to be hit often, was adamant he would not smack. Conversely the six-year-old believed strongly that smacking is a necessary and positive part of helping children grow into responsible adults, *'I thought about what Timmy said – that you shouldn't smack children – yeh we might say not to be bad but if they've been bad...or if the other parents don't care yeh – other mummy's or dads don't care when they hurt others – if they don't care, they might become a burglar when they be big'.*

A six-year-old boy said, *'I would smack children when I'm at the age of 20 or an adult because if I'm a parent you have to smack children'.* When he was asked why he thought parents have to smack children he replied, *'because if you smack children when you're an adult it tells them not to do the same mistake again'.*

There was concern among children about the effects of parents smacking children, children then smacking their children and adults, and this practice continuing unchecked into future generations.

> *'It depends on what the law is then but...sometimes when I get really cross I will smack them but I think I would just try to get them out of the habit. I don't really want to do it so the child doesn't do it to other people'.* (seven-year-old girl)

> *'No, because I think smacking is not very nice and I when I grow up I hope my children will be nice. And I'm not gonna smack them because I don't want to smack my children because say when they grow up and they can still remember that day when they got smacked...and then they'll start a fight...and they'll smack little children'.* (seven-year-old boy)

> *'Because it's mean and it hurts the child and they'll just learn to smack people and they'll go on and it won't help at all'.* (seven-year-old girl)

> *'...I wouldn't smack any of my children anyway because they will just start smacking other people and if I smack someone then they are going to start smacking other people, because they think grown ups do it and if the law didn't allow smacking I would just send them out to their room and let them have a think about it'.* (seven-year-old girl)

Children who said they would not smack when they are adults said they hoped and planned to have positive relationships with children. A five-year-old girl explained, *'because I'm going to make friends with the little child and I'm going to take them to the park or a party or a disco'*; another five-year-old said he wouldn't smack *'because I want to be friendly'*. A seven-year-old suggested that, *'it depends what the law is of course and it depends on what your children are like, as if they were really good like Imogen, Francesca, Oliver and Harry at school...I don't know what they are like at home, but at school they are very good. If I had children like that I wouldn't need to smack them'.*

When you are big, will you smack children: key themes and discussion points

Half the children who answered this question said they will not smack children when they are big. Five and six-year-olds were noticeably less keen on the idea of them smacking as adults.

This may be related to the fact that younger children are more frequently hit (Newson and Newson, 1989; Smith, 1995), and are therefore more 'in touch' with how it feels to be hit. It could also suggest that as children grow older they begin to rationalise and accept that smacking is a normal feature of relationships and that children deserve to be hit. This is understandable as the alternative 'world-view' open to children who are hit is to believe that their parents are doing something wrong, and by association, deliberately setting out to hurt them.

When you are big, will you smack children?
A selection of quotes from children

When you are big, do you think you will smack children?

No, because it's not a good thing to do

'No, because I don't like it' (five-year-old girl)

'No, because I don't want to and I might hurt them which I don't want to do, so I'll just shout at them' (seven-year-old boy)

'No, because it's not nice to and it hurts the child's feelings' (seven-year-old boy)

'No...because I don't like smacking children' (five-year-old girl)
'No' Why not? *'Because it's not going to be a very good idea'* (five-year-old girl)
'Because I want to be friendly' (five-year-old boy)
'No, because it's nasty' (five-year-old boy)
'No, because it isn't very nice' (six-year-old girl)
'No, cos it's nasty and you go in a huff and they hit you' (six-year-old boy)
'No...because it's too bad for them...because they're crying and they always do it' (six-year-old boy)
'Because if I hurt someone and they didn't hurt me I wouldn't hit them' (six-year-old boy)

It Hurts You Inside

'No' Why not? 'Because it's mean and it hurts the child and they'll just learn to smack people and they'll go on and it won't help at all' (seven-year-old)

'No, cos it's horrible and you make your children cry' (seven-year-old girl)

No, I'll do something else instead

'No only if they be, I'll only punish them if they be naughty...I'd tell them not to I'd tell them to go by the wall until two hours or I might say that..."you should think about what you've done – all the bad things". And if they've been naughty I might say "next time you do that I'll give you a bad punishment, I'll take all your money away from your pocket."' (five-year-old girl)

'I would send them to bed' (seven-year-old girl)

No, because I feel sorry for them, and like them

'No' Why not? 'Because sometimes they're good and I feel sorry for them' (five-year-old girl)

'No. Well, most children I like. Especially ones younger than me who are only about three or two. Most of them I know and I like them and I'll know my own child' (six-year-old girl)

'I think I won't smack children because they'll be a bit nice and they'll sort of be better than evil children' (seven-year-old girl)

No, because it is against the law

'No...because you'll get put in jail' (five-year-old boy)

No, because it could be dangerous

'No...because if you smack them and you try to get them they'll run away from you and they'll go on the main roads' (six-year-old girl)

No, because it will cause more violence

'If you smack children because they're doing something they might get very angry and slap you on the face [and the adult] would get angry and slap you back' (six-year-old girl)

'No' Why not? 'Because then, then when they grow up, they'll smack their children. And those children will smack their children and it will carry on and on and on' (seven-year-old girl)

Yes, when they are naughty or bad

'Yes because they're going to be naughty...They will hit each other' (five-year-old boy)

'Yes' Why? 'When they're naughty' So what kind of things will you smack for? 'When they hit me, when they push the books from the library [if] she broke mum's glass and she jumped in from the window and the dad said to mum it was danger' (five-year-old girl)

'When I don't like people [adults]...Only when they're [children] naughty to me' (five-year-old boy)

'If they're my own children, I'll smack them if they're naughty' (six-year-old girl)

'Yes, because if they get naughty, you have to do the same' And what kind of things are naughty? 'Stealing, getting new clothes muddy' (six-year-old girl) Yeh because they might be naughty at their mum or dad or their friends – they might beat up somebody else' (six-year-old)

'Yes, when they're naughty' What kind of things will they do if they're naughty? *'Throw glass, throw stones, pinch people, kick'* (six-year-old boy)

'I'll smack the children when they're naughty, like if they throw stones at a house and they keep throwing it and people walk along and they might throw it at the person' (six-year-old girl)

'Yes, when they swear at you [and] if they kick you and if they don't get in the car and if they spill my cup of tea over [or] if they shout at me [or] if they draw all over my bedroom' (six-year-old boy)

'I think if the child gets naughty, really really naughty, I'll smack them' What kind of things would a child do to be really naughty? *'Throw stones, because it might go on a car or, like, get a pipe or stone and go like that and it might go on a car'* (six-year-old boy)

'Not a lot' If you will a little bit, what do you think you'll smack them for? *'If they're being naughty'* So what kind of things? *'Like if you broke a bed'* Anything else? *'Like they have a sister or brother and they've just done a model and they stamp all over it'* So, if you deliberately break something? Nods (seven-year-old girl)

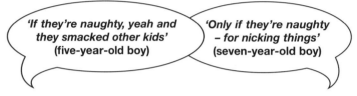

'If they're naughty, yeah and they smacked other kids' (five-year-old boy)

'Only if they're naughty – for nicking things' (seven-year-old boy)

'Only if they're naughty: smacking grown ups, spitting chewing gum on the carpet, and going to the shops and other places they're not allowed' (seven-year-old girl)

'Only if they're like really, really naughty' So what would be really, really naughty? *'Like breaking something that was really valuable and worth a lot of money and knocking something down like a dress or a table'* (seven-year-old girl)

'Only if they're naughty – if they spit their chewing gum on the carpet' (seven-year-old boy)

'Only if they're naughty' And what kind of things would be naughty? *'If they broke something or ripped somebody's shirt'* (seven-year-old boy)

'If they're naughty, I would smack them' What kind of things are naughty? *'Like, [if you throw] a stone and it hits the window and it smashes it'* So it's about breaking things? *'Yes, and if it hits a car or a van or a vehicle'* (seven-year-old girl)

'Sometimes' Sometimes, and what would be the reason? *'If they had a ball what was new and they threw it over the next door neighbour's fence, and we couldn't get it back because they might be on holiday. It might have to stay there until they come back, and I'll give them a smack then'* (seven-year-old girl)

'If they're naughty I will' So what kind of things would you smack for? *'If they say swear words to me [or] write all over the walls in my room [or] erm, spill all my coffee and throw Mars Bars on the floor and rip the real flowers up'* (seven-year-old girl)

'Yeh, erm when they pull faces at me and put their middle fingers up at me [and] like when we're playing cricket when I win they might be mardi' (seven-year-old boy)

Yes, if the child is crying for nothing

'Not often' Not often. So, if you would sometimes, what kind of things do you think you'll smack for? *'If they don't stop crying and if it's nothing to cry about [and I've said] "stop it" already and they start crying for nothing'* And you think if you smacked them, it would help? *'No'* (seven-year-old boy)

Only sometimes if they really get on my nerves

'No – sometimes when they're really really getting on me nerves but not as hard as adults do. [You might get hit] when your mam throws some paper out and you go in the bin and say "mam can I have this bit of paper?" and she says "no, because they're all things in the bin that are out of date and you might catch diseases"' (seven-year-old girl)

Yes, because parents *have* to smack children

'I would smack children when I'm at the age of 20 or an adult because if I'm a parent you have to smack children' Why do you think you have to smack children if you're a parent? *'Because if you smack children when you're an adult it tells them not to do the same mistake again'* Do you think you could do anything else instead of smack them so they didn't do the same thing again? *'Yeh punish them'* Punish them? *'Like you can stop pocket money and they have to go to bed as soon as they come home from school and no supper'* (six-year-old boy)

It depends on the law

'It depends on what the law is then but...sometimes when I get really cross I will smack them but I think I would just try to get them out of the habit. I don't really want to do it so the child doesn't do it to other people' What if the law said you couldn't smack? *'I wouldn't do it'* (seven-year-old girl)

'It depends what the law is. If it was no, you weren't allowed to smack, I wouldn't smack any of my children anyway because they will just start smacking other people and if I smack someone then they are going to start smacking other people, because they think grown ups do it and if the law didn't allow smacking I would just send them out to their room and let them have a think about it' (seven-year-old girl)

It depends on what the child is doing

'I think it depends what the child is doing. If they are good you don't really need to smack' (seven-year-old boy)

Q9a. Do you know anybody who doesn't like smacking?

Who doesn't like smacking?	Frequency no. of different children who gave this answer
Me	24
Dad	22
Mum	21
Friends	17
Grandparents	11
Everyone in my family	5
Cousins	5
Aunties	5
All children	5
Policemen/ambulance/fire brigade/postman	5
Uncles	4
Brothers and sisters	4
All grown ups	3
Don't know anybody who doesn't like smacking	3
Teachers	2
Teddies/toys	2
Animals	2
Splodge	2
Nanny (carer)	1
Babies	1
Santa	1
Jesus	1
Nobody on this table (in this group)	1
You and Tina (project workers)	1

The most commonly mentioned sets of people who children thought do not like smacking were children themselves followed by dads, mums and friends.

Most of the children were able to list adults as people who don't like smacking; only one group of six and seven-year-olds could not think of any adults they know who don't like smacking. They did, however, dislike smacking themselves, and named many friends. A seven-year-old explained:

> *'Me, because it hurts very very much and you could just say to the children go in your bedroom for a few hours and watch the tele' and later I'll have your tea ready.'*

Her classmate added:

'My friend – she's six – cos when she bes naughty she always gets smacked and she doesn't like it. And I don't like getting smacked either because it hurts so much.'

Five children said that all children don't like smacking while three said 'all grown ups'. A couple of seven-year-olds gave thought-provoking answers to this question; a boy said Jesus doesn't like smacking while another proclaimed Santa not to like it *'because he's a good man'*. A five-year-old girl listed the project workers as people who don't like smacking, perhaps indicating that we were showing our disapproval in our body language, or general manner. Alternatively, this child could have assumed that only adults who reject smacking would be motivated to visit children to hear their views on the subject.

A five-year-old girl explained how smacking can be physically painful for the person smacking too, *'my mum doesn't like smacking cos if she does she'll just have to do it again and again and her hand will get sore and she won't like it she won't be able to cook with it and do stuff'*.

Do you know anybody who doesn't like smacking: key themes and discussion points

Children listed themselves, parents and friends as the main people who don't like smacking. This is interesting as it shows that, from their perspective, the people who don't like smacking the most are a) those who are hit most often, and b) those who hit the most.

This question raised the possibility of bias in that two children thought that the central character *Splodge* in the story book disliked smacking, and another child suggested that the two project workers do not like smacking. We cannot draw any firm conclusions from children's observations as the vast majority made no comment about the project workers' views on smacking. In any consultation process participants will make assumptions about those carrying out the consultation (see section 10), and there is always the possibility of responses being affected by these assumptions.

Do you know anybody who doesn't like smacking? A selection of quotes from children

Do you know anybody who doesn't like smacking?

Me!

'Me because it hurts and you go in a huff' (six-year-old boy)

'Yes, me. Because every time you get smacked it hurts your feelings' (six-year-old girl)

'Myself, my dad, my mum, my sister' (five-year-old boy)
'I don't like smacking...I don't like mum or dad smacking. I don't like my mum and dad smacking' (five-year-old boy)
'Me because it hurts very much and you just go in a huff and go upstairs' (six-year-old boy)

'Me and my sisters' Are they big or little? *'One's a bit bigger and one's a bit smaller'* (six-year-old boy)

'Yeah, me. Because I might just get told off by someone and I don't want to' (six-year-old boy)

'Yes, me. Grown ups that are cross with me but they only smack me a few times when they're extra cross with me' (six-year-old boy)

'I don't and I know somebody else who doesn't. One of my friends, Anthony and there's Jessica Grey who doesn't go to this school. She's in a different school' (six-year-old girl)

'Me but sometimes I do smack because my brother gets on my nerves I don't mean to smack but sometimes my brother gets on my nerves a bit and I don't know what to do' (seven-year-old boy)

'Me, because it's not very nice' (seven-year-old girl)

'Me, because it hurts' (seven-year-old boy)

My dad

'I don't think my daddy likes smacking, he doesn't really want to' (seven-year-old girl)

My mum

'My mum doesn't like smacking' (five-year-old girl)

'My mother not too much, but if she really has to then she would do it but she doesn't really smack people unless they have been really naughty and they were told off ten times for doing the same thing and my dad doesn't like smacking at all and I don't think anybody on this table likes smacking either' (seven-year-old girl)

My friends

'Nicola doesn't, Jane doesn't, Rosie doesn't' (five-year-old girl)

'My friend doesn't like smacking because if she gets smacked [by another child] she'll get a sad face and if she does it three times she'll get a sad face and she'll go up to Miss and get in the incident book' (five-year-old girl)

'My friend and my cousin and another friend' (five-year-old girl)

'My friends – I don't know anyone else' (six-year-old boy)

'Yes' Who do you know? *'Amy'* Is she a grown up or a child? *'A child. When we went to the park she got smacked'* (seven-year-old)

'Some of my friends, because it hurts' (seven-year-old boy)

'All my friends' And why do all your friends not like smacking? *'Because it hurts'* (seven-year-old girl)

'My best friends don't like smacking, because when they've smacked they know that the person they've smacked is going to tell the teacher' (seven-year-old girl)

'Nobody in my family does like smacking because they think it is wrong to hit the child because when they grow up they might smack their children' (seven-year-old boy)

Everyone in my family

'My mummy, my daddy and my nanny and all my family and probably my friends. I don't like smacking either' (seven-year-old girl)

'Yeah. My mum doesn't like smacking, which you know sometimes she can't do everything. My dad doesn't smack and he doesn't like it. I don't know about my sister, my granny and grandpa don't. They know that it is not very good because grown ups are in charge of us. I don't like smacking and I don't like being smacked either' (seven-year-old girl)

'My mum and dad, Francesca's mum and dad and lots of people like all my relations' (seven-year-old girl)

My cousins

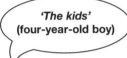

'Me cousin [who's five] doesn't like smacking because she screams and says the f-word' (six-year-old girl)

'My cousin, because when he wants me to play with him he doesn't smack my sisters or anyone. He doesn't like it' (six-year-old girl)

'Me' Anybody else? *'My mum and dad, my grandparents. And my cousin. I've got lots of cousins but there's only one that doesn't like smacking'* Right. And is that cousin a grown up or a child? *'A child, cos I'm the biggest cousin'* (seven-year-old)

My aunties

'My aunties, my animal, my teddies' (five-year-old girl)

Children don't like smacking

'The kids' (four-year-old boy)

'Somebody who doesn't like getting smacked – children' (six-year-old boy)
'Me, my friends and all children' All children? *'Even adults'* (six-year-old boy)

Lots of people don't like smacking

'My dad, my nan, my granddad, my cousin, my friends, my teddies, my Barbie' (five-year-old girl)
'Fire brigade, the ambulance, policemen, your nanny, your daddy, your grandad, your mummy and your nanny, your mama. Or your sister, or your uncle' (five-year-old boy)
'Mums and dads, grandmas, aunties, nannas, grandads, uncles' (five-year-old boy)
'Me, my mum and dad, all the children I know don't like smacking' What about any of the grown ups? Do you know any other grown ups who don't like smacking? *'All those children's parents'* So do you know a lot of people who don't like smacking? *'Yeh'* (seven-year-old)
'Sophie' Is she a grown up or a child? *'A child. And Martha'* Is she a child? *'Yeh. And Rebecca'* Another child? Yes? *'And my mum and dad. And me. And my auntie and uncle, my cousins and my grandpa and grandma'* (seven-year-old)

Grown ups don't like smacking

'Grown ups. Even parents' (seven-year-old boy)

Babies

'The baby, when you smack your baby they cry and the baby doesn't like the sister or your mum anymore because you smack your baby' (five-year-old girl)

Adults in my family...and you!

'My mum, my dad, my auntie, my nan and you and Tina' (five-year-old girl)

Teachers don't like smacking

'Your teacher and your family'
'The teachers' (seven-year-old boy)

'Your mums and dads and Splodge' (six-year-old girl)

Splodge

'Splodgy!' (six-year-old boy) I think you're right, but Splodgy hasn't said so. But maybe after listening to you all, it will make up its mind.

Q9b. Who thinks it is wrong to smack?

Almost all the children who answered this question (66 from 72) said smacking is wrong. Many referred to smacking generally rather than simply assuming we were only asking them whether it is wrong for adults to smack children.

Only four children said it is OK and another two were unsure:

> *'I think it's right and wrong because if dogs are naughty you have to smack them.'* (seven-year-old boy)
> *'I think it's good and bad because when you've been naughty it teaches you not to do it again.'* (seven-year-old girl)

Children gave various reasons why it is wrong to smack:

Reasons why smacking (anybody) is wrong

Smacking is wrong because: it hurts; it is painful; people do it too hard; you could do something else instead; it makes people cry; it makes people [adults] run away; it's bad manners; it's embarrassing; it makes children go in a huff; it's a bad thing to do; adults can smack very hard; it might stop your blood for a few minutes; it could hurt the bones; it sets a wrong example for other people; you could damage something; you might get a bruise or a lump; it's horrible; you might fall; you might feel very poorly; you may have done something by accident such as spill your parent's tea or coffee.

One group of seven-year-olds said they had informed their friends they would be talking about smacking that afternoon. They told us that two boys had told them they liked being smacked. The group of children proceeded to tell us they didn't believe their friends. A girl explained,

> *'I don't think they like being smacked – the children – they just say it. Because they think they are big and not afraid of anything, I mean I don't think anybody would like being smacked at all...they probably don't like smacking they just say it, it's a joke and they say they are not afraid of anything.'*

The vast majority of children who answered this question said they thought smacking is wrong. There were no noticeable differences between age groups, and those that said smacking is OK were evenly split across groups. This suggests that children were not subject to undue peer pressure to give the majority response to this question.

It is interesting that significantly more children said that smacking is wrong than said they would not smack children when they are adults. This could have been because this question was asked in a less neutral way than the one about future smacking. Alternatively, it could suggest that children – like adults – know it is wrong to hit but nevertheless manage to rationalise physical punishment as an acceptable and necessary part of parenting.

We accept that this question was leading as it asked people to identify themselves as having a particular opinion rather than us asking them to share their views. It also followed a question which asked children to identify people who don't like smacking.

When preparing the story book we discussed this question a great deal, and tried to think of different ways of asking the same question. In the end we opted to continue with this question for two reasons. First, we could not produce an alternative which was straight-forward and in tune with the conversational nature of the story book (see section 10). Second, the way we asked the question encouraged children to qualify their replies rather than simply saying 'me' or placing their arm in the air, as most did initially.

Who thinks it is wrong to smack?
A selection of quotes from children

Who thinks it is wrong to smack?

It's wrong because you could do something different

'Wrong because you could do something instead' (five-year-old)

It's wrong because it hurts

'Because they go in a sad face' (four-year-old boy)
'Cos it really hurts' (five-year-old girl)
'Because when you smack children it hurts like when my mum tells me off and she feels like she's going to slap me and she doesn't slap me she just tells me and says "Letitia go into your room and stay in bed until you apologise"' (five-year-old girl)
'Yes, because when we smack they cry, the people cry then other people smack you so they run away and never come back so they have to find another family or [live] in another country. The helicopter puts him with another family' (five-year-old girl)
'Because it hurts' (five-year-old boy)
'Because people could start crying' (five-year-old girl)
'Yes, because you start to cry...and they get sent to their room' (five-year-old boy)
'Cos it really hurts you if they smack you' (six-year-old girl)

'Me cos when you get smacked it hurts so you go in' (six-year-old girl)

'Wrong, because you might fall or someone might be pulling you and the other person might smack you and that place might hurt you very much' (six-year-old boy)

'My mummy thinks it is wrong to smack because when people do it's...sometimes too hard and sometimes the child goes straight up to bed and lie on the bed until it is time for supper and they don't come down for supper' (seven-year-old boy)

'It will give you a pain. It might stop your blood for a few minutes' (seven-year-old girl)

'It's painful' (seven-year-old girl)

'It's painful and it can hurt them and it could hurt the bones' (seven-year-old girl)

'Because some people get hurt and they might have a bad bruise or they might have a stitch and it might hurt' (seven-year-old girl)

'I think it's wrong because you might get hurt and you might get a bruise or a lump. And it's horrible' (seven-year-old girl)

'When you're smacked, you might have a very big cut and you might feel very poorly and you might have a stomach ache and they might smack your stomach and it might feel even worse' (seven-year-old girl)

It's very wrong to smack

'It's very wrong to smack, because it's very very very very very bad manners' (five-year-old girl)

It's wrong because it's embarrassing

'Me, because they always go in a huff and they always get embarrassed when they tell their friends [they've been smacked]' (six-year-old boy)

'Because someone will get very very embarrassed when you go in a huff and ask for something and the person who's there will get very very mad with you an' all but they get embarrassed because they don't want to say anything they go beetroot red. It's more embarrassing in the house because you can fit loads of people in the house. And when I get smacked I get very embarrassed' (seven-year-old girl)

'[It's embarrassing when your friends find out you've been smacked] because they might think it's funny' (seven-year-old girl)

It's wrong because it's a bad thing to do

'Because a smack is a very, it's not a very bad thing, but it's a bad thing to do' (six-year-old boy)

It's wrong to smack when children have accidents

'If somebody goes like that and there's coffee there and the mum and dad just turn around and they're looking at the floor like that and they don't know if he's done it by accident then they just come up to him and smack him when it wasn't his fault he just went like that by accident and knocked it over' (seven-year-old boy)

Lots of people in my family think it's wrong to smack

'I think everybody in my family thinks it's wrong to smack as well. Apart from you know some people... lets say [if] the person next door likes smacking then – if the law changed – I don't think that they will be very cross although they think it was wrong to smack. I think they would just forget about the whole thing. And I think it is wrong to smack and everybody in the family thinks so' (seven-year-old girl)

'I think it is wrong to smack, my mum thinks it's wrong to smack, and my dad thinks, and my grandparents probably don't smack, but my mum and dad would do it if they really had to' (seven-year-old girl)

It's wrong because it encourages more violence

'I think it is wrong to smack but, it could be painful because if you do it to another person they might do it to another person and it might carry on until everyone is smacking which won't be very good' (seven-year-old)

It's OK because it's only gentle

'Shakes head – Because they just go like that [gentle tap on leg]' (five-year-old girl)

It's OK to smack because you have to discipline children

'I think it's OK to smack because if you don't smack when you're an adult your children will follow you and if you don't smack, your children will not have any discipline' (six-year-old boy)

It's OK to smack because it teaches you not to do it again

'I think it's good and bad because when you've been naughty it teaches you not to do it again' (seven-year-old girl)

Q10. How can we stop children being smacked?

How to stop children being smacked	Frequency no. of different children who gave this answer
Children don't be naughty/be good/be nice	31
Parents do other things/don't hit for accidents/behave better	22
Change the law/tell adults to stop smacking/just stop them	13
Tell parents how it feels	5
Children hide from parents	4
Children buy adult a present	3
Tell the Prime Minister/the Government	3
Other adults intervene when children are being smacked	1
Ring the police	1
Write a book	1
Write a prescription for mums and dads	1
Child to persuade their adult not to smack	1
Child to pretend they're already hurt	1
Adults be nice to children	1

Most children interpreted this question as meaning what could they, or their parents, do to stop smacking. Children were not asked about changing the law, although a small number did mention it.

The ideas and suggestions children gave to stop children being smacked were split between what adults – mostly parents – can do, and what children can do to stop or reduce smacking. On most occasions children began by focusing on their own behaviour and there was great emphasis placed upon the need for children to be good and not naughty. A seven-year-old girl explained that,

> 'You could stop children from being smacked by children being kind and not naughty, and doing things that are right.'

Her classmate gave the following advice:

> 'Stop being cheeky to your mam and stop telling lies and don't cause trouble with the other kids because then your mam will tell the other mam and they'll have an argument and you will cause an argument and if I tell lies I get a hiding and a smack.'

A five-year-old boy said that 'children can be nice' and a six-year-old boy declared, 'you should always be good and never shout at your mum and dad and be naughty and always nick the money'. A seven-year-old girl remarked that we can stop children being smacked 'by being good for all your life'.

One seven-year-old boy who spoke graphically about being hit by his parents said that if children do well at school then this may prevent them being hit:

'Er, stop being bad and...being good in class and getting stuff in assembly and getting stuff from your teachers and all that kind of stuff and doing good work...and one day I finished my language yeh all of it and my teacher was very pleased with me so she gave me two stars and my mum was very pleased.'

Children were not viewed as the sole people responsible for ending smacking; many children said that parents can act differently. Suggestions included parents sending children to their room, verbally instructing children to stop what they are doing and encouraging children to behave positively through rewards. Children in one group believed that if parents understood what it feels like to be smacked then they would stop. A seven-year-old girl suggested, *'we could tell them how it feels and if we do something naughty then they could make you stop it by telling them in words'*. Two girls, when asked whether they thought parents didn't already know how it feels to be smacked, replied:

'They might have been smacked when they were little, they were brought up with smacking them so they think it's right to smack.'

'They might remember being smacked but not really remember how it feels because it seems so long ago. And as they got older when they thought about it they forgot how it feels.'

How to stop smacking: key themes and discussion points

The children we listened to clearly accepted major responsibility for ending smacking. The overwhelming message was that children believe that if they stop being naughty then adults will stop smacking. This begs the question: is smacking doing anything to help children behave better? If children are right, and it is their behaviour that has to change independently of adults, then this not only makes smacking redundant but also greatly reduces the role of parents in helping children develop and grow into healthy and responsible citizens, now and in the future.

What is more likely is that children have internalised very strong messages from adults that they are smacked because of their own actions rather than any responsibility resting with their parents.

This question prompted children to offer a range of ideas and insights into how children can be encouraged to behave well through positive actions on the part of parents. Such actions included talking and reasoning with children, using rewards and encouragement and employing non-violent sanctions such as withdrawing 'treats'.

How can we stop children being smacked?
A selection of quotes from children

If children stop being naughty/if children be good

'If they be good all week and all month...they won't get smacked' (five-year-old girl)

'If the adults ask children to do it and the children do it' (six-year-old girl)

'Don't be naughty by getting dressed and not telling lies' (five-year-old girl)

'Help like tidying their bedroom up' (five-year-old boy)

'Stop being naughty' (five-year-old boy)

'Well, I think a good way is that the children if they usually do something else sometimes do things with their parent, they won't have to get smacked because they both want to do it or something and they're allowed. Then they won't get smacked and if the rest of the time when they want to play other things they could do it with their other friends. And if they're not allowed to they could just play in their bedroom doing something on their own. So they won't get smacked. Because if they don't get in the way, they won't be able to get smacked' (six-year-old girl)

'By not being bad' (six-year-old)

'Being good and do what you're told to do' (six-year-old boy)

'By being kind and good' (six-year-old boy)

'[Adults can stop smacking] if the children don't be nasty' (six-year-old boy)

'By stop doing the naughty things' (six-year-old girl)

'If the children don't be naughty, then they'll stop smacking' (six-year-old girl)

'By being very good and not pulling people's hair or pushing off bikes' (six-year-old)

'Start to be good' (six-year-old boy)

'They can stop smacking other people, then their mum won't smack them' And what could adults do? 'They could say, "stop smacking the other one and then you won't get smacked"' (six-year-old girl)

'You have to be good, then you'll not get smacked' And what could adults do? 'They might say, "if you be good we'll not smack you"' (six-year-old boy)

'Children should be staying out of mischief and be kind' (seven-year-old girl)

'To do things that they should' (seven-year-old boy)

'To do what they're allowed to do' (seven-year-old boy)

'Because they can just stop doing things naughty and they'll not get smacked any more' And what could adults do? 'By telling them to not do it again and they might say if you do it again you might get sent to bed' (seven-year-old girl)

'Not be naughty, not wander off with somebody' (seven-year-old boy)

'By being good. If children be good they won't be smacked. If they be bad they will be smacked. Be good.' (seven-year-old boy)

Parents can do something else instead

'By making them feel good' (five-year-old girl)

'Take your toys away' (five-year-old boy)

'Say "stop this" or be nice or say "don't do that" or go and tell the teacher' (five-year-old boy)

'[Grown ups could] stop pulling faces when children are not looking and nicking all their pocket money' (six-year-old boy)

'Say "don't do that, please"' (six-year-old boy)

'Tell them not to do naughty things...and say don't be naughty and send them to bed' (six-year-old boy)

'The grown ups can tell the children to tidy up their bedroom and do that because they don't want to get smacked any more' (six-year-old girl)

'Because adults don't want to have to hit children all the time...they could just say "you go in the kitchen and I'll sit in the sitting room for a little while and then you can come back in we'll talk about it"' (seven-year-old girl)

'[Adults could] try not to smack them' (seven-year-old girl)

'By telling them to be good' (seven-year-old girl)

'By telling them not to do it again' (seven-year-old boy)

'By telling them to do things that the grown ups say they can do' (seven-year-old boy)

'[Adults can] tell them to go to bed' (seven-year-old girl)

'[Adults can] shout instead' (seven-year-old girl)

'You could ground them instead' (seven-year-old boy)

'[Grown ups could] stop smacking them: just send them to bed' (seven-year-old boy)

'If you just...shout at them for a while and they're being naughty and you've just told them to stop, they might do. But if you smack them or something they probably won't, they'll do more stuff. But if you just do it for about two more weeks and there's time to stop being naughty...you will [stop them being naughty] because you don't really want to be smacked all the time' (seven-year-old boy)

> 'Yes, you can either say "stop it" or "enough of this fooling around" or "go to your room and stay there until you apologise"' (five-year-old girl)

> 'If [they] do an accident stop, don't smack them' (seven-year-old girl)

> 'You can stop children being smacked if you tell them and tell them and tell them and warn them and [then] they won't [be naughty]' (five-year-old girl)

> 'Say "can you please stop doing it?"' (six-year-old boy)

Change the law, tell adults to stop smacking and give information to parents

'I don't know...try to stop our parents smacking – try to make sure they don't smack ever again [tell them] to stop smacking' (five-year-old)

'Write a letter and put it in the post' Who would we write a letter to? 'To your children' To your children and what would you say? 'I'm sorry to be smacking you and you say to your children you're a nice little child and we wouldn't smack you ever again' (five-year-old girl) 'Send them [parents] a letter' (five-year-old boy)

'Tell the adults' (six-year-old girl)

'Stop it. Tell adults to stop it' (six-year-old girl)

'We can stop children being smacked by going round with letters saying to stop children being smacked, stop adults being smacked and it is against the law to' (seven-year-old boy)

'If it is against the law and if people who are in special organisations and link to have the right to say to put posters up in places saying... "please can you stop smacking children"' (seven-year-old girl)

> 'I think you could put it on the news' (seven-year-old boy)

'[Big people like the interviewers could] write a book about trying not to be naughty so you can help the mams and the children not to smack' (seven-year-old girl)

'You could write a prescription and send it to your mam and write on what we said and put on "very important – don't smack children on the head because you might cause brain damage"' (seven-year-old girl)

'I was just thinking that if they changed the law then a lot of people will realise what they had done to their child and they would probably...be happy that the law was changed. If they don't change the law they will think "oh well, the child doesn't mind so we can keep on doing it"'. But if they realise that children have been talking to adults about it then I think they will definitely realise that it hurts their child and they will be very upset with themselves' (seven-year-old girl)

Children tell parents how it feels

'By telling the parents how you feel' Anything else we could do? 'Make the children not be naughty' (seven-year-old)

'Tell their parents how it feels and you could smack them instead' And then what do you think would happen, if children smacked parents? 'They would get angry and they wouldn't talk to you till the day after' Do you think that would help, if parents got smacked, do you think it would help children not be smacked any more? 'Not sure' (seven-year-old girl)

'Well, you could persuade your adult to stop smacking. Or you could stop being naughty' How could you persuade your adult to stop smacking? 'By saying or pleading' Would you say anything special to your adult? 'Please' (seven-year-old boy)

> 'Well, you can say, "well, how would you feel if somebody bigger came up to you and smacked you?" And say things like that and [say] "it doesn't help at all because you're just going to make it worse"' (seven-year-old girl)

> 'Tell your parents how it feels and tell the parents to make the children be good' (seven-year-old)

Children can hide

'By hiding' (five-year-old boy)

'But if they hided, they wouldn't get smacked' (seven-year-old boy)

Children can buy their parents a present

'You could buy them a present or you could give them a necklace if you find one' (five-year-old girl)

'The children buy sweets for their mum or dad or they can buy them a toy or a necklace' (five-year-old girl)

'Buy them a present or a book' (five-year-old girl)

Tell the Government

'By telling the Government, the prime minister, and doing what you are doing mainly and just, let's say people wrote to the Government or the Prime Minister about why they don't like being smacked and they think it is wrong to. Then they probably will have to change the law and it would be on the news, and if you really like and if you don't like being smacked then tell the Government and it depends how many people think it's wrong to be smacked' (seven-year-old girl)

'I think it is my grandfather – or my god father – and he is in the House of Lords and I think if somebody wanted to tell the Prime Minister but they couldn't get that close they could always tell someone in the House of Lords' (seven-year-old girl)

'We could do it by [telling the] Prime Minister [or you] could just tell someone important in the law – someone like a Lord' (seven-year-old girl)

Somebody can stand in the way of a parent who is about to smack

'You can do this (puts arms up in air) and your mum can be there and the man will be there [and you will] split them up... then [the child] sits down and have a drink and then she gets tucked into bed' (five-year-old girl)

Ring the police

'I know – ring the police and your auntie can say stop' (five-year-old girl: putting hand up)

Children can pretend they are already hurt

'Pretending that they've already been hurt a real lot. And pretend they've got a broken arm like I have' (six-year-old boy)

8. Contrasting beliefs about smacking

Despite the widespread nature of smacking, it remains a taboo subject. Those individuals or organisations who attempt to open up debate often find themselves ridiculed or pilloried.

Smacking is one of those subjects which hits a deep nerve, it provokes strong, emotive responses from people on both sides of the fence. Even people who are sitting on the fence – those that have never properly considered *why* as a society we routinely hit children – can quickly muster up potent arguments in defence of smacking. In this section we consider the main findings from our consultation exercise and compare them with commonly held adult attitudes and views about smacking.

Children talking about smacking – the main messages

- Children defined smacking as hitting; most of them described a smack as a hard or very hard hit.
- Children said smacking hurts.
- Children said that they are the main people who dislike smacking followed by parents, friends and grandparents; the vast majority of the children who took part thought smacking was wrong.
- Children said that children respond negatively to being smacked, and adults regret smacking.
- The children said parents and other grown ups are the people who mostly smack children.
- The children said they usually get smacked indoors and on the bottom, arm or head.
- The children said the main reasons children are smacked include: they have been violent themselves; they have been naughty or mischievous; they have broken or spoiled things; or because they have disobeyed or failed to listen to their parents.
- The children said children do not smack adults because they are scared they will be hit again; adults do not smack each other because they are big and know better, and because they love and care about each other.
- Half the children involved in this consultation exercise said they will not smack children when they are adults; five-year-olds most often said they will not smack children when they are big.

In order to compare children's and adult's beliefs it is necessary to list some commonly held adult attitudes and views which are relevant to our particular findings:

Relevant commonly held attitudes and views among adults:

- smacking is not the same as hitting;
- smacking does not hurt;
- adults know how to smack safely;
- children need to be smacked to avoid hurting themselves;
- adults smack children when they are under pressure in public spaces;
- smacking is a good way of disciplining children.

We will now take each belief in turn and contrast it with the messages from this particular consultation exercise.

Adult belief – smacking is not the same as hitting

The belief that smacking is not the same as hitting is strongly defended by many adults who prefer instead to describe a smack as a 'gentle tap' or a 'loving slap'.
This consultation exercise found: In **all** our group discussions, children said smacking was hitting.

Adult belief – smacking does not hurt

Many adults pass off smacking as something which doesn't really hurt children. When they do acknowledge that smacking hurts children, they say it is only temporary and has few long-term effects.
This consultation exercise found: that children *are* hurt when they are smacked, both physically and mentally. Children gave graphic accounts of the effect of smacking; they also explained in detail why they do not smack adults – because they are too small and cannot hurt adults as much as they can hurt them. The impression from this consultation exercise is that smacking *does* have harmful consequences: two seven-year-olds explained that smacking makes them feel like they don't like their parents anymore; one even said she felt like running away.

Adult belief – adults know how to smack safely

Those who believe in the existence of 'safe smacking' commonly assert that most adults hit children in 'safe' areas of the body, or use only 'reasonable force'.
This consultation exercise found: A significant number of children, when asked where on the body do adults smack, mentioned the head area. Another three said adults smack children anywhere on the body. In other parts of the group discussions, children referred to adults being stupid and hitting them on their heads 'where they're not supposed to'. In the course of all the group discussions only one child said his response to being smacked was to laugh – all the others said it made them cry.

Adult belief – children need to be smacked to avoid hurting themselves

This belief centres on a perception that adults only ever smack children when the children are facing immediate danger, or to prevent them being harmed. Typically those who reject smacking are accused of being prepared to allow young children to run into roads, or place their fingers in electrical sockets or gas fires for example.
This consultation exercise found: Only six out of 76 children said children are smacked when they place themselves in potentially dangerous situations: playing in their dad's van; going off without prior permission; talking to strangers; and touching a hot cooker or light bulbs.

Adult belief – adults smack children when they are under pressure in public spaces

Adults often excuse the widespread practice of smacking children in public spaces as an understandable response from parents under pressure. They explain that in public spaces parents often feel driven to smack children because other adults are watching and critical of their child's poor behaviour. The belief is that other adults expect parents to smack.
This consultation exercise found: The children involved in this exercise said most smacking takes place indoors at home, or in other adult relatives' houses. Nine participants talked about children being smacked in shopping centres while another described being hit by his mum for laughing while in a queue for a Lottery ticket. Eight of these ten children said parents tried to hide the fact they were smacking children. The children believed parents did this to spare their own and children's embarrassment; and to avoid negative interference from onlookers. This suggests, from children's perspectives, that sometimes adults are ashamed of smacking children, and that adults sometimes recognise the humiliation involved in smacking children.

Adult belief – smacking is a good way of disciplining children

This view suggests that smacking is an important component of 'good parenting'.

This consultation exercise found: The children were not asked if smacking made them better or worse behaved, but the impression from this consultation exercise was that smacking succeeds in interrupting children's behaviour but has many other associated negative effects. Many children proposed that smacking could be stopped by children behaving better; none of them suggested that this might be difficult to achieve without smacking. While many children did say they would smack when they were adult, the vast majority of the whole group said they thought smacking was wrong; and none argued that smacking could not or should not be stopped.

Although there were children who said that children 'be good' or try to make amends after they have been smacked, the general responses suggest that smacking has a range of harmful consequences: children said they did not like their parents anymore, that they felt angry, upset, grumpy and sad after being smacked; and a significant number said smacking made them 'be more naughty'.

9. Responding to children talking about smacking

This report speaks to all adults. However, there are three particular groups who have most to learn from children talking about smacking: parents; children's organisations and professionals working with children; and the Government. The distinction between parents on the one hand and professionals and Governments on the other, is a crude one as clearly they are often the same group of people. Professional and political debates and views about smacking are often informed by adults' experience of being parents, and we hope that those who work with and on behalf of children will address what they can do next as parents as well as professionals.

Parents

We didn't propose children should exclusively talk about parents – they could have easily directed their discussions at other adults who smack children. From very early on in this exercise it was clear that smacking is most associated with parents, and that parents have the most to learn from listening to children.

The principal messages from children were smacking is wrong, it hurts, and parents smack because they are bigger and older. Indeed, a significant proportion of the children we listened to said children do not often retaliate because they are scared of being hit back by their bigger and stronger parents.

The children we listened to were pragmatic; many said they understood why parents feel they *have* to smack. They also told us that many parents quickly regret hitting children, and that smacking is more of a habit than a carefully thought-out way of coping with stressful or irritating situations.

Children had many useful suggestions about how parents can stop smacking. They advised parents to talk more and use other methods such as grounding, removing treats and sending children to their bedrooms. Some suggested that letters should be sent to parents telling them to stop hitting children; others were sure parents would stop if they 'knew how it feels'; one seven-year-old suggested a 'prescription' should be drawn up to help her parents stop hitting.

This consultation exercise confirmed professional and common-sense judgements that smacking does nothing to enrich children's relationships with parents. We heard that smacking makes children feel cross, sad, frightened, embarrassed, naughty *and it hurts*. One seven-year-old explained that it makes her dislike her parents; another of the same age said she feels like running away when she is smacked; and a seven-year-old boy described the anguish of waiting for his father to return home from work to be informed he had 'been bad'. Other children described parents as 'silly' or 'stupid' for hitting children on the head.

On many occasions during this piece of work we were struck by how odd it all felt. Here we were, two grown adults, talking to representatives of a group of people who are routinely hit to ask them to tell us what it feels like. The same situation with other groups of people – say women or adults with learning difficulties – would be unimaginable. That is because our society views hitting any adults as socially or legally unacceptable (although there exists high levels of violence between adults, especially from men towards women). Why is it OK to hit children? Is it because children are seen as a different class of people?

Throughout this consultation exercise, children were very open about their perceived failings. Without prompting, they spoke in detail about the types of behaviour which usually result in children being smacked. Mostly this involved children themselves being violent or nasty – kicking, biting, pinching for example – but other examples included swearing, accidentally knocking things over, breaking things and playing with friends who their parents disapproved of. As our exercise progressed it appeared that children could be smacked for almost anything. A lot seemed to rest on the parent's mood at the time; many of the children involved described parents as being very angry, cross or red in the face when they smacked children.

It is startling that so many children are hit because they themselves have hit. It is hard to accept that parents, in these instances, are helping their children develop more appropriate ways of resolving conflict. The picture we gained is that parents act more in retribution than positively setting out to increase children's awareness of the consequences of their actions. If parents habitually magnify their children's acts of violence, what message are they sending to children? That all forms of violence are unacceptable; or that it is OK to hit if you are bigger, stronger and have more power than your victim?

There were a range of non-violent actions which children described which, if carried out by adults, would not be dealt with in the same way. Adults accidentally spill drinks, linger over tidying their bedrooms and spend time with friends who others see as a bad influence. When children do these things they are hit; why do we seem able to tolerate and understand bigger people doing these things, but not children?

Being a parent carries great responsibility and many parents struggle to provide the best for children despite the pressures of poverty, unemployment, lack of adequate support and poor housing. There are particular dynamics to parent-child relationships which can cause great stress and pressure for adults. Children can be emotionally very demanding and require a high degree of physical care. These factors are present in some adult-adult relationships for example, adults with severe learning difficulties, Alzheimer's disease or recovering from a stroke but nobody condones them being hit.

In the end our discussions with children lead us to conclude that the reason children are hit is because they are not really seen as individual people. As a seven-year-old girl explained, *'adults are bigger and stronger and people treat them more seriously'*.

Children's organisations and professionals working with children

Children's organisations have a pivotal role in supporting and, advocating on behalf of, the six million under eight-year-olds across the UK (ONS, 1998).

None of the children involved in this consultation exercise mentioned children's organisations by name. They did, however, offer a range of suggestions which children's organisations could act upon. First, there is a need for educational campaigns – in children's words this should include putting up posters; giving out leaflets and letters to parents; and making a news broadcast to let people know smacking children is wrong. Second, there is a need for continuing support to parents to help them develop non-violent relationships with children. As a five-year-old explained, *'try to stop our parents smacking – try to make sure they don't smack ever again'*.

There is another lesson for children's organisations and professionals working with children: that young children have much to contribute even in seemingly taboo areas. On a simple, practical level children's organisations, and professionals working with children, could commit themselves to further ensuring that the young children they are in contact with have meaningful and varied opportunities to contribute to all areas of policy development and decision-making.

The Government

There are two principal messages to come from this report to Government. First, children need the same legal protection from physical assault as adults. Throughout this consultation exercise children repeatedly referred to smacking as hitting, and explained in great detail the damage caused by smacking – on them physically and emotionally, and on their relationships with parents. Second, children's experiences of smacking must be part of the debate on physical punishment and the Government's consultation process. This consultation process shows the hurt and suffering caused to children – and to relationships between parents and children – by smacking. The children we listened to found no distinction between smacking, hitting, slapping and whacking. They used these interchangeably. Some children talked about 'hidings' and one child mentioned the use of canes; three children talked about children being locked in their rooms. Although all the children talked about parents smacking children, teachers, nannies, babysitters and foster carers were also mentioned as people who smack children.

It is no surprise that most children interpreted our question about stopping smacking as being related to the actions of themselves or parents. Some children – from the independent school we visited – did talk about writing to the Prime Minister and the Government. Others focused on the need for children and adults to behave better.

Clearly governments cannot wait for their youngest citizens to lobby them before taking action on their behalf. Children, because of their lack of power and experience, need assistance to communicate their views and experiences. The National Children's Bureau and Save the Children have listened carefully to 76 young children talking about smacking. We have now passed their views and experiences to those who are in a position to act; as a seven-year-old girl optimistically noted, *'...If there is a lot of people, like I don't know, 70 or something then I think he [Tony Blair] would definitely change the law'*.

10. Lessons in listening

Context

There are increasing numbers of projects and initiatives where children's voices are heard and their opinions sought on matters which affect their lives (Cohen and Emanuel, 1998; Save the Children 1998; Treseder, 1997; Willow, 1997).

The National Children's Bureau and Save the Children are always striving to develop new ways of helping children and young people be heard. This particular project was a challenge to us in two main respects: first we had to successfully engage with very young people; and secondly, the subject we wanted to consult about was potentially upsetting to children. It wasn't until we had completed the first pilot discussion that our concerns were laid to rest and we were again reminded that adults can often wrongly predict children's responses and reactions. In fact few of the children we listened to displayed any form of upset or discomfort during the discussions.

Age and competence are crucial when considering the rights of the youngest children to be heard. While many would not question the right of older children to have their views taken into account, the views of younger children – in this case, children under the age of eight – are often thought to be unreliable.

There are several reasons for this; two are perhaps worth considering in some detail:

- the idea that young children are somehow incompetent;
- difficulties finding out what younger children think.

Young children and competency

The views of Piaget, Inhelder and other developmental psychologists have had a powerful influence on the way we think about children and childhood across Northern Europe and the United States. Working in the 1920s, Piaget suggested through a series of simple experiments, that young children between the ages of two and seven are 'egocentric' and unable to take on the perspective of others.

These findings have been revised by researchers such as Donaldson (1987) and Dunn (1988), who have provided powerful evidence of young children's capacity to put themselves in the position of others and to empathise, given an understandable and meaningful context.

Nevertheless, young children are still seen as incompetent and irrational, just as women used to be viewed. And very much as was the case with women, children are frequently considered unable to exercise sound judgement in relation to their own lives. Despite this, there are increasing examples of young children making rational and informed decisions in some limited areas hitherto closed to them (Alderson, 1993; James, 1995; Malek, 1995).

For instance, the work of Priscilla Alderson (1993) on children's consent to surgery illustrates that children as young as eight can take decisions about options for their own medical treatment. As Alderson explains, *'children become competent by first being treated as if they are competent'*. There are other examples of children being able witnesses in courts of law (Morrow, 1996).

Why are adults unable to accept that children are competent? As Morrow suggests, *'disparities in power and status between adults and children'* lead to the questioning of children's competence. Children, when compared to adults in their communities, clearly have less experience and knowledge, but this does not detract from what children do know.

It is vital to respect and recognise young children's competencies; but also to acknowledge that children are not all the same. This understanding alone on the part of adults will go some way towards a more effective way of working with and listening to children.

This consultation exercise indicates that children have considerable understanding and insight into their own and other people's behaviour and feelings.

Finding out what children think

Berry Mayall (1994) in Morrow and Richards (1996) argues that *'though the representation of children's views may be only partially accurate and may be mediated by the adult researcher's concerns and interests, the attempt must be made to forward children's interests'*.

The main challenge to adults is to find a range of ways of communicating with children to enable them to express their views and opinions. As Lansdown (1995) says, *'we do not have a culture of listening to children'*. She outlines a framework for listening to children, which includes some of the following points:

• ensuring that children have adequate information appropriate to their age with which to form opinions;
• providing them with real opportunities to express their views;
• listening to children's views and considering them with respect and seriousness;
• telling children how their views will be considered;
• letting them know the outcome of any decision.

Judy Miller in *Never Too Young* (1997) makes similar points. In a range of situations children can exercise successful decision making and express their views on matters that affect them. To do so they need information; the opportunity to express their views; to have those views taken seriously and to be clear about what happens next.

Viewing children as competent and listening to them, Miller argues, empowers them to make informed decisions within early childhood settings – about the food they eat, the way their day is structured, how budgets are spent, and in some cases about staff recruitment.

Listening to young children talking about smacking

The starting point of this project was that very young children have a basic human right to be heard on matters which affect them. Our organisations also believe that the competence of young children is too readily underestimated or dismissed.

In establishing a framework for these views to be expressed, we sought to ensure that ethical and practical issues about the best ways to work with children were addressed, and that the children's views were properly sought and represented.

Recruitment

It proved difficult to gain access to children. It was especially hard to find schools and centres that wanted to take part in the study. Head teachers, teachers, school secretaries – the gatekeepers – were often concerned about how they thought parents would react. We were told that many parents would be extremely unhappy for their child to discuss such a subject with people from outside agencies.

It was also suggested that some parents would feel particularly threatened because of past involvement with social services. Other concerns were that as the children were so young, it might be easy to 'put words into their mouths'. It was apparent that schools and centres did not want to 'stir up trouble' among parents by even broaching the subject.

However, once agreement was given for parents to be approached, a number of parents in every school/centre did give permission for children to take part. This varied from four children in one school to 20 in another. Parents were approached by letter, distributed by the school or the centre (see Appendix A).

Because the groups were 'self selected', the groups of children we listened to cannot be considered to be representative. Nevertheless, only two children from a group of 76 said that they had never been smacked.

Informed consent

On arrival in the school or centre, children were usually sent through to the area where the discussions were to take place. At this point, although parents had given permission and the children knew about the project, they had not personally agreed to take part.

Informed consent from the children was considered critical by the project workers. Time was spent at the beginning of each session explaining who we were, and that we wanted to hear what children thought about smacking. We also told them that if they agreed to take part their words would be included in a report (we used the term book). It was further explained that the book would be given to the Government (people like Tony Blair – whom most of the children had heard of). Children were also told that if they did not want to take part they did not have to, that we would stop at any time, and switch off the tape recorder.

There was also a discussion about how we could make sure that everyone had a turn to speak. Children usually suggested that each person in the group take a turn to speak.

Time was also spent stressing that there were no right or wrong answers and that it was important for children to express their own thoughts, not to copy their friends.

Children were also reminded that if they wanted to talk about smacking after we had gone they could talk to a member of staff, usually the person who sat in the session with us.

To stimulate discussion and help enable the children talk about general experiences (as well as their own if they chose), a story book featuring the character Splodge was used.

Using the story and its illustration helped us maintain children's attention. A few older children questioned the method, confirming our suspicions that direct questions would be more convincing for people over the age of eight. But Splodge appealed to the children we talked to, despite its unattractiveness to many adults!

It is perhaps worth noting that it is difficult for children to truly give consent in the school environment. The experience of school for most children is of a place where consent is not commonly sought, and that there is an understanding that children comply with the adult agenda.

The environment

In one open plan school the discussions were held in a part of the classroom. This proved too much for the majority of one group of five-year-olds who asked to end the discussion as they noticed drinks and biscuits being distributed. Working in a quiet room without distractions, preferably not during play time worked best.

Why group discussions?

We chose to use group settings to listen to children to compensate for the power differences between children and adults. Given that most parents smack children, we felt that children in one-to-one settings might be inclined to understate their feelings or experiences of smacking for fear of upsetting or contradicting the views of the adult questioner.

We also wanted to avoid giving any impression that these discussions were aimed at questioning individual children about their personal experience of physical punishment. Had we used one-to-one interviews we fear that not only would children have been daunted by the prospect, but also that parents would inevitably become suspicious about our motivations.

The questions

The questions themselves seemed to be pitched at the right level for this age range, although a seven-year-old boy did query when we were going to ask him *a hard one*.

There is some evidence from child development studies that young children have a sophisticated ability to try and second guess why adults are asking questions. Using a story board with a naive character to ask questions is one way to overcome this, encouraging children to enter into the spirit of the story and provide useful information.

Having said this, it was apparent in some cases that while we made enormous efforts to try not to influence children by never revealing our own views on smacking, children did (probably more than we realised) detect our position on smacking and perhaps this affected their responses. The fact that we were asking questions at all about the subject, as well as the style and the content of the questions, probably enabled children to establish our positions without much difficulty. Nevertheless, children appeared able to stick to their own opinions without being overly influenced, demonstrated by the number who said 'yes' to the question about whether they will smack when they are adults .

Children's responses

Children tended to shift from reporting their own experiences to speculation about what happens to children in general, sometimes in the same sentence. While this might be slightly confusing to the reader we believe that *all* the information children had to report is of interest in that it represents both their experiences and perceptions of smacking.

We deliberately set out to construct an exercise where children didn't have to dwell on their own memories of what might be potentially very unpleasant experiences, especially in groups with adults they hardly knew. Therefore using Splodge as a naive questioner enabled children to choose whether to talk about their own experiences or to think about smacking in general.

While the question and answer format is more often used in one-to-one interviews, it did not seem appropriate to interview children singly about smacking. This would have meant that each child would have the focus of two adults (interviewer and teacher/worker). As smacking is a potentially upsetting subject it was felt that the group afforded children more privacy. It might however be interesting to develop this consultation project further by using the Splodge character in one-to-one interviews with children and familiar adults.

The question and answer format tended not to generate discussion. Children generally were patient while they waited for each other to answer questions. The story book helped to maintain a steady pace and interest in the proceedings, with most children looking forward to finding out what was on the next page.

It is hard to assess whether children were influenced by the replies of their peers. As is the case in any group it is inevitable that thoughts and ideas will be generated by what has gone before. It is our view that this is no more the case with a group of children than it is with a group of adults.

What do children understand by smacking?

Smacking describes a range of experiences. For instance, in one school 'smacking' is a locally used term for beating up, and is often used in the playground; therefore in this school 'smacking' can refer to what children do to each other. Even so children still listed adults as the main group that smack.

In other answers it appeared that children were putting themselves in the position of the person who smacks rather than the recipient. Having said this, the majority of the answers appear to refer to smacking in relation to what adults do to children.

Interpretation of the responses

All the group discussions were tape recorded and then transcribed. Responses to each question were then broken down into separate points and coded into categories as reproduced in the tables. The aim was to give a rough indication of the range and frequency of the responses.

The literature on child development is full of instances where adults interpret children's behaviour and responses. In this consultation exercise there is an element of interpretation. This cannot be avoided, but the words of the children themselves form the heart of the report.

Differences between children?

This was not a research study and it was not the intention to set out to find differences in what children think about smacking according to age, gender, ethnicity and region, although all these factors will have a bearing.

Impressions of the project workers was that gender, region and ethnicity did not present as big issues. Nevertheless, differences in children's responses according to age were noticeable. The most significant difference was that younger children appeared less accepting of smacking, and – unlike older children – did not perceive their own behaviour as being the primary cause of smacking.

Issues of child protection

Child protection concerns can be raised in any group of children talking about physical punishment. We spent a lot of time preparing for this, and were clear that these discussions must never veer into forums for individual children to share in detail their personal experiences or concerns. However we also did not want children to be silenced if they had worries they wished to discuss. One of the primary reasons we asked a member of staff from each school or play scheme to observe the discussions was that it allowed us to point out to children that here was a 'friendly adult' who they could talk to if they wished.

It was made clear to parents in the parental consent form that the school would follow normal procedures if necessary. Children taking part were also told that if they felt they wanted to talk a bit more after the session, then they could talk to someone whom we had previously identified, usually the member of staff sitting in with the group. As far as we are aware this never happened.

During the course of the group discussions if issues were raised that gave any cause for concern (for instance, the evident distress of one child who was a witness to violence in the home) then this was noted and we ensured that the member of staff sitting in the session had taken note too. For the two group discussions held without a member of staff present, the school/centre was subsequently contacted and concerns passed on.

What next?

This consultation exercise is a snap-shot of what groups of young children in different parts of the country think about smacking. As noted elsewhere in this report, smacking is a common experience in the lives of most children. As yet we have very little information from children themselves about what it feels like to them, or what can be done to work towards a non-violent society. It is hoped that this project will encourage others to seek out the views of children. We have a lot to learn from listening to them.

References

Alderson, P (1993) *Consent to Surgery*. Open University Press

Cohen, J and Emanuel, J (1998) *Positive Participation: Consulting and involving young people in health-related work. A planning and training resource.* HEA

Creighton, S and Russell, N (1995) *Voices from Childhood*. NSPCC

Donaldson, M (1987) *Children's Minds*. Fontana Press

Dunn, J (1988) *The Beginning of Social Understanding*. Basil Blackwell

Ghate, D and Daniels, A (1997) *Talking about My Generation*. NSPCC

Hakansson, G (1996) 'The Effects of Sweden's Ban on Physical Punishment', *Journal of Child Centred Practice*, 3, 2 (Nov), 17-27

Hodgkin, R and Newell, P (1998) *Implementation Handbook for the Convention on the Rights of the Child*. UNICEF

Hood, S, Kelley, P and Mayall, B (1996) 'Children as research subjects: a risky enterprise', *Children and Society*, 10, 2 (Jun), 117-128

James, J (1995) 'Children speak out about health', *Primary Health*, 5, 10, 8-12 (Nov/Dec)

Lansdown, G (1995) *Taking Part, Children's Participation in Decision Making*. Institute for Public Policy Research

Lansdown, G (1995) *Building Small Democracies. The Implications of the UN Convention on the Rights of the Child for Respecting Children's Civil Rights within the Family.* Children's Rights Office

Malek, M (1995) 'Counselling with young children', *Children UK*, 6 (Autumn) 4-5

Miller, J (1997) *Never Too Young: How children can take responsibility and make decisions.* National Early Years Network and Save the Children

Morrow, V and Richards, M (1996) 'The ethics of social research with children', *Children and Society*, 10, 2 (Jun), 90-105.

Mayall, B (*ed*) (1994) *Children's Childhoods Observed and Experienced*. Falmer Press

Newell, P (1989) *Children are People too: The case against physical punishment*. Bedford Square Press

Newson, J and Newson, E (1989) *The Extent of Parental Physical Punishment in the UK.* APPROACH

Nobes, G and Smith, M (1997) 'Physical punishment of children in two-parent families', *Clinical Child Psychology and Psychiatry*, 2, 2, 271-281

Office of National Statistics (ONS) (1998) *Key Population and Vital Statistics: Local and health authority areas*. ONS

Save the Children (1997) *All Together Now: Community participation for children and young people*. Save the Children

Smith, M A (1995) *Community Study of Physical Violence to Children in the Home and Associated Variables*. Poster presented at the 5th European Conference, International Society for the Prevention of Child Abuse and Neglect

Treseder, P (1997) *Empowering Children and Young People: training manual*. Children's Rights Office and Save the Children

UNICEF *United Nations Convention on the Rights of the Child* (available from UNICEF, 55 Lincoln's Inn Fields, London WC2A 3NB)

Willow, C (1997) *Hear! Hear! Promoting Children and Young People's Democratic Participation in Local Government*. Local Government Information Unit

Appendix A

What do children think about smacking?

Information for parents and carers

In November 1997 the Government announced it would be consulting widely on physical punishment. They plan to do this because the European Commission of Human Rights ruled last year that the law in this country failed to protect a child who was repeatedly hit by his step-father.

The National Children's Bureau and Save the Children think it is really important that young children have a chance to let the Government know their views. That is why we have set up this unique project.

What is the project about?

The project will give small groups of five to seven-year-olds a chance to give important information and advice to the Government and other adults. They will be asked to:
- describe what a smack is
- say what it feels like to be smacked
- explain why, when and where children are smacked
- give advice on what could be done to reduce or stop smacking

As a token of our thanks, each participating school will receive £75 book vouchers.

What the project is not about

The project will **NOT** encourage children to talk about their own experiences at home. We want children to give us general advice and information rather than talk in detail about their personal experiences.

If a child does want to talk about any personal experiences her/his school will follow normal procedures.

Who will talk to children?

The group discussions will be led by Carolyne Willow from the National Children's Bureau and Tina Hyder from Save the Children. Carolyne and Tina have worked with children for many years and have lots of experience of helping children express their ideas and views. A member of staff from your child's school will be present throughout the group discussions.

When will the discussions take place?

The small group discussions will take place sometime in July. They will take about 30 minutes. We will arrange the dates and times with your child's school to make sure they do not affect normal lessons and activities.

What will happen to the information?

We would like to tape-record the small group discussions to make sure we gather *all* of the children's advice and information.

When we have finished all our discussions (we plan to visit five different schools) we will write a report which will be published by the National Children's Bureau this autumn. Your child's school will get a copy of this report.

We plan to write about the project in newspapers and magazines. It is very unusual for young children to give advice to the Government and other adults so we want to get as much publicity as possible.

We will not include names of children who take part, or the names of schools, in anything we write.

For more information contact:

Carolyne Willow
National Children's Bureau
Telephone Nottm 0115 960 8089

Tina Hyder
Save the Children
Telephone London 0171 700 8127

Parent/carer consent

Please complete this tear-off slip and pass to your child's headteacher

I agree that _____ (name of child) can take part in a small group discussion about smacking.

Name of parent/carer
_____

Signature
_____

Date
_____

Please note: we will only involve your child if they **and** you give your consent

Appendix B
The Storybook

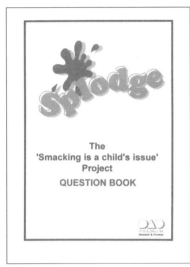

**The
'Smacking is a child's issue'
Project
QUESTION BOOK**

This is *Splodge*

HELLO !

Nobody knows where *Splodge* comes from.

Splodge does not know very much about our world. *Splodge* is always asking questions.

Do you think you can help *Splodge*?

Today *Splodge* has been thinking about smacking and would like to know what YOU think about it.

Are we ready to begin?

Splodge has a question,

Who knows what a 'smack' is?

Splodge asks,

Why do you think children get smacked?

Splodge asks you to think,

Who usually smacks children?

Splodge now asks,

Where do children usually get smacked?

Splodge now wonders,

What does it feel like to be smacked?

Splodge has two more difficult questions,

How do children act after being smacked?

How do adults act after they have given a smack?

Splodge wonders,

Adults smack children but why don't children smack adults?

Children smack each other but why don't adults smack each other?

Splodge wants you to think,

When you are big, do you think you will smack children?

Splodge says,

Do you know anybody who doesn't like smacking?

Who thinks it is wrong to smack?

Splodge has one more big question,

How can we stop children being smacked?

Splodge has to go now,

Thank you for helping me with my questions,

BYE!